The Creativity Algorithm

HOW TO REACH YOUR SALES AND PROFESSIONAL GOALS WITH APPLIED CREATIVITY

JOSEPH SWOPE, PhD

Praise

"Finding out-of-the-box solutions is more important than ever for today's leaders. Swope's book can help people think differently."

— Jim MacPhee, Author
Engage, Inspire, and Lead: Riding the Waves of Life and Leadership from my 43-Year Career at The Walt Disney Company

"This is a book you will highlight, flag, and underline many times over. Beautifully written and brimming with amazing information, it will fire up your creative spirit and change your life as never before."

— Anthony D. Fredericks, Ed.D., Author
Two-Minute Habits: Small Habits, Dynamic Creativity

"Creativity can feel like a lot of things, but this is the first book I've read that makes it feel like a skill anyone can learn. And I can't think of a single person in any job that wouldn't benefit from some of these exercises."

— Josh Erikson, Author
Ethereum Earth Series

"For nearly 30 years my digital media company has helped some of the world's largest and most successful brands infuse creativity into marketing and sales. Dr. Swope's framework on the creative process is unique, innovative, and game-changing. This book is a must-read for a corporate executive who seeks to energize growth at their company."

— Marc Hausman, President and CEO,
Strategic Communications Group, Inc.

"Thinking strategically requires creativity. The Creativity Algorithm can help with improving creative thinking."

— Patrick O'Donnell, Partner,
Harris, Wiltshire, Grannis Law Firm

"Finding different ways to connect with people often requires different ways of thinking. This book provides insightful ways to successfully help with that."

— Melanie Porpiglia, Senior Consultant
and Master Trainer PI Midlantic

To John and Barbara Swope who unfailingly
encouraged me to explore and create.
You are models of support and love.

To Heather, Arden, and Madeline,
continue to learn, create, and make the world better.

Special thanks to
Charlie Fritts and Anne Fulton-Foley-Brunner
who slogged through the first version of this book.

Thanks!
Joe

Copyright January 2025
by Joseph Swope Phd

Publishing in the United States
by Ingram Content Group

This book cannot be reproduced in any form without explicit permission from the author.

ISBN-13: 979-8-218-47363-1

Contents

How to Use This Book 1
Exercise 1: **Introduction to the Creativity Algorithm** 3
Exercise 2: **Sculpt the Mind** 9
Exercise 3: **Gathering Legos** 15
Exercise 4: **5D Printer** 21
Exercise 5: **Don't Chase Puppies** 27
Exercise 6: **How Many Numbers Are There?** 31
Exercise 7: **Afterthoughts** 37
Exercise 8: **The Point of Relaxing** 43
Exercise 9: **Defining Creativity** 47
Exercise 10: **Academic Definition** 51
Exercise 11: **Plant Another Garden** 57
Exercise 12: **What Comes First?** 63
Exercise 13: **Big C and Little C** 69
Exercise 14: **Train Yourself** 75
Exercise 15: **Building Robots** 81
Exercise 16: **Comfortable Doing Nothing** 87
Exercise 17: **Thinking with Muscles** 93
Exercise 18: **Out-of-Shape Personal Trainer** 99
Exercise 19: **Is DWI Unsafe?** 105
Exercise 20: **Daydreaming in Class** 111
Exercise 21: **Bowling Balls and Blankets** 117
Exercise 22: **Impatient CEOs** 123
Exercise 23: **Christmas Vacation** 129
Exercise 24: **Muscular Bag of Acid** 135
Exercise 25: **Filling Out Forms** 141

Exercise 26: **Musical Norm** 147
Exercise 27: **Control Room** 153
Exercise 28: **Control Room, Part 2** 159
Exercise 29: **Sleep Jerk** 165
Exercise 30: **Mulch Barrier** 171
Exercise 31: **Teenage Wine** 177
Exercise 32: **Tomato Cage** 181
Exercise 33: **No More Steps on the Ladder** 185
Exercise 34: **Word Games** 191
Exercise 35: **Paddling to Sleep** 195
Exercise 36: **Writing a Letter** 201
Exercise 37: **Fast-Moving Stream** 207
Exercise 38: **Writer's Block** 211
Exercise 39: **Three Pages of Powering Through** 217
Exercise 40: **Mowing the Lawn** 223
Exercise 41: **Dropping Kids Off at Camp** 229
Exercise 42: **Smoke Leaf** 235
Exercise 43: **Uncovering Naked David** 241
Exercise 44: **Off-Course Runner** 247
Exercise 45: **Good Sore** 253
Exercise 46: **Zoomies** 257
Exercise 47: **Flooded Carburetor** 261
Exercise 48: **Handful of Sand** 265
Exercise 49: **Sweet Release** 271
Exercise 50: **What if** 277
Exercise 51: **Bigger Batteries…** 281
Exercise 52: **Best Song Ever** 285
Afterword 291
Endnotes 293
References 303

How To Use This Book

It's been said that business success and other professional goals are only one good idea away.

This book is your guide to finding those innovative ideas more often. It is a compilation of fifty-two independent exercises, one per week for a full year. At the end of each exercise is a takeaway, a fun, little challenge which, if done regularly, will help you achieve that goal.

As organized as that might sound, you can always feel free to skip ahead, jump backward, or read in any order. Each exercise is a stand-alone practice, although Exercise 1 (Introduction to the Creativity Algorithm) is a must read first, as it details the premise of the entire book.

Reading through each exercise, you may also see some explanations more than once. That's OK. Repetition is the mother of learning.

This book is not a quick fix for your creative thinking. Instead, it teaches you 'the long game'. That analogy refers to planning and taking actions with a focus on achieving long-term success rather than seeking immediate results. It means the ideas you have now may not pay off right away but are expected to bring positive benefits in the future. Perseverance is the key here. Still, it is possible to have a career-changing great idea after only one exercise.

Keeping notes is important, so have a notebook handy to jot down your thoughts as you read. There are a few blank pages at the back of the book where you can start, but I believe those will fill up quickly. As you have more and more thoughts, each of those thoughts can become a starting point for a cascade of even more thoughts. In that case, using an electronic log would be ideal.

My last piece of advice is to enjoy this book. It will be a fun learning experience. Innovative ideas don't—can't—won't—arrive when you are stressed or don't like what you're doing.

So, enjoy and always remember...

Your success is only one innovative idea away.

Exercise 1

INTRODUCTION TO THE CREATIVITY ALGORITHM

The Creativity Algorithm seems like an oxymoron, like it can't possibly exist. Isn't creativity supposed to be wild and unpredictable, not a step-by-step process that anyone can follow to have their next innovative idea?

Well, yes and no.

THE NATURE OF CREATIVITY: DEFINING THE INDEFINABLE

Like many things in psychology, creativity is not definable, and is also difficult to simply think about. While we might not have a perfect understanding of creativity, this book offers a process that is based on observation, hypothesis, and, hopefully, many supporting data points that *you* will collect as a result.

I *could* start this paragraph using the phrase, "the process begins with...," but that's like saying a circle begins with a certain point. Having a good idea is not a linear process. It doesn't have a starting point any more than your mood has a starting point. If you think a bad mood starts with an external event, consider that if you were in a different state of mind when that event happened would it have bothered you? Yet, your state of mind is dependent on your mood. If that sounds too complicated, look at it this way:

> *You think as you feel, but your thoughts determine those feelings.*

ALPHA STATES AND SOPHISMS: KEY CREATIVITY ALGORITHMIC TERMS

It might not be accurate to say that creativity *begins* with a person entering the so-called "alpha state" of consciousness. It is accurate to say that innovative ideas almost always happen when a person is in an alpha state.

Alpha and Beta Waves

An alpha state is named for alpha waves, the first brain waves to be discovered using electroencephalography (EEG)[1].

The second type of brain waves to be discovered were named beta. Beta waves are most associated with concentration and with the conscious mind. Beta concentration can be an obstacle to having good ideas. Stress, overthinking, and ruminating are all done in a beta state.

Alpha waves are mostly associated with dreaming, daydreaming, and musing on nothing and everything. The mind is engaged, but not focused. An example of this is an artist, musician, or athlete being in the zone. They are not consciously thinking about what they are doing. In fact, they are not consciously present at all. Their mind is in a so-called "flow state[2]" where they are simply moving the paintbrush, creating the music, and playing the game. In fact, if artists or athletes start to consciously think about what they are doing, they seem to bump themselves out of the zone.

Once in an alpha state, you can begin to work on cognitive puzzles that we'll call sophisms. A sophism is a pleasant mental challenge or exercise that flexes and stretches the mind. It is technically defined as an *"argument for displaying ingenuity in reasoning or for deceiving someone."* For the purpose of the Creativity Algorithm, we are not trying to deceive with sophisms—we are trying to distract. Specifically, we are trying to distract the conscious mind so that we can more easily enter the alpha state. The technical-sounding term for this is *open monitoring meditation*[3]. The important thing to remember is that playing with a sophism and being in an alpha state is not merely pleasant—it's *fun*.

Sophistic Examples

Having established the key terms of alpha state and sophism for our purposes, it is perfectly reasonable to ask whether playing with a sophism will help you achieve an alpha state or if getting into an alpha state will allow you to play with a sophism. If that is a bit confusing, just imagine a chicken hatching itself from an egg it laid right before it hatched from it.

That right there—thinking about the chicken and egg—was a sophism. Let's look at another example of the type of sophism that will be used with the Creativity Algorithm. Before we do, take a deep breath, enjoy it, and let it out slowly. That will help you shift into an alpha state.

Now, for a moment, just a moment, try to *envision* an inverted bubble. Now, picture the process of turning the bubble inside out. Did you do it? Did you do it without popping it?

Before your conscious mind actively focused on envisioning it, your subconscious mind woke up and became interested. It is that sliver of pure curiosity that precedes what we want to make routine for ourselves. The deep breath and the enjoyment over the weird thought allowed you to get closer to an alpha state and to the point where innovative ideas arrive.

If you could rewind what just happened in your mind, you'll find it is amazingly similar to what you felt before you had your last good idea. If you can't remember that exact moment, it's OK. Most people don't. It's that moment that we want to practice.

What Does This Have to Do with Helping People Reach Their Professional Goals and Have Revenue-Generating Ideas More Often?

THE CREATIVE ALGORITHM HYPOTHESIS AND PROCESS

Now that we have a basic understanding of the terms and components, let's look at the hypothesis and process that the Creativity Algorithm is based on:

> 1. If a person is relaxed while they engage their mind with a sophism, then they will enter an alpha state that will help the arrival of a good idea.

> 2. If a person regularly plays with sophisms and regularly enters an alpha state, they will have transformational ideas more often.

Just like artists and athletes, accountants, managers and sales professionals can get stuck. They can find themselves on a plateau with no obvious way to climb to the next level. Still, it only takes one transformative idea to break free and get to the next level. The exercises in this book allow people a way to get to that next level.

TAKEAWAY FOR THIS WEEK

> Remember the notebook that I recommended from the How To Use the Book Section? Grab it and have it handy. Sit down, relax a bit, then try to remember the last time you had a good idea or felt in the zone. Compare that with the feeling you had when you were playing with the concept of the inverted bubble. If you can't find a memory to compare, reflect on how you felt when you were playing with the sophism of the inverted bubble. A few moments of flexing and stretching the mind can be all that is required to help your brain change. After you do that, give your subconscious brain some time to process; you will be impressed by what it brings you.

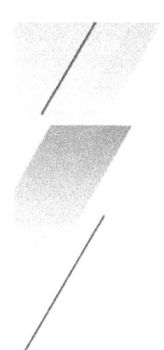

Exercise 2

SCULPT THE MIND

Have you ever been in a class where the professor was nervous or it seemed like he didn't know the subject matter? Did it make you cringe with social discomfort? I have been in a class like that. It was awful and, unfortunately,

I was that professor!

The class was introductory psychology. The word "psychology" is defined, in simple terms, as the study of the mind. I knew what "study" meant. The problem was and still is the fact that I actually don't know what the mind is and I don't think you do either.

On the first day of that class, I gave the students an extra-credit challenge—I asked or maybe even *dared* them to sculpt a model of their mind.

That is a pretty good sophism. If you skipped the introduction to this book or the first exercise, *a sophism is a relaxing creativity exercise that can help you flex and stretch your mind*. Stop reading for a few minutes, take a deep breath and try to conceptualize how you would make your own mind sculpture.

What Does This Have to Do with Helping People Reach Their Professional Goals and Have Revenue-Generating Ideas More Often?

GETTING UNSTUCK

If you tried, even for a few seconds, to think of doing that assignment, you would be one step closer to the part of your mind that offers you innovative ideas. That attempt at pushing your mind in a new direction is an important part of the process of finding more efficient solutions or finding new ways to make money. Getting unstuck requires creativity and creativity is a skill that must be practiced. Thinking about what color(s) the mind is or how big the mind is an indirect way learning the skill.

The goal of this book is to help people and companies (which are comprised of people) learn the strategies and techniques that will help them coax innovative solutions from the subconscious. This is not a motivational book, nor is this a self-improvement exercise with mantras and platitudes. It rests on a hypothesis and evidence-based premises. The hypothesis is that if you *regularly* practice the exercises in this book, then you and the people of your organization will have more frequent contact with transformative ideas. This can help increase sales and productivity.

The crucial technique is:

To engage in cognitive exercises called sophisms while you are relaxed.

Skeptical? Collect the evidence yourself. After trying a few weeks of the exercises in this book, see if you notice a greater connection with the part of your mind that offers you revenue-generating ideas.

You've had good ideas before. Probably lots of them. But oftentimes it seems like having a good idea is akin to seeing a shooting star—rare, amazing, and seemingly out of your control We can never have total *control* over when a good idea arrives, but we can have *influence* over when it does. Imagine having influence over how often inspiration comes to you!

At the instant of inspiration, everything seems possible, and the different levels of the mind are synchronized. For that brief instant, we are at our best. I want to help you have that feeling more often, more regularly, and more predictably.

Process and Product

This exercise—and, in fact, this whole book—is *process-oriented*. It advocates a type of enjoyable and healthy mindfulness that focuses on *seeking*. Whether a good idea arrives on time does not affect how you feel when you are inviting it.

THE TWO-HANDLED SPOON

This exercise is also *results-oriented*. It focuses on *finding*. We live in a world that values product over process. Our jobs and personal lives require solutions. Our managers don't really care that we enjoyed the process if we didn't get the task done. The previous paragraph described how the seeking and arrival of a new idea is great by itself. But what if that new idea is the concept of a two-handled spoon? The process might have been fun, but that great idea is probably not valuable unless you are the producer of a children's TV show or Ripley's Believe It or Not.

Spoon Usage

Here's another sophism for you. Take a deep breath, enjoy the inhale, and let it out slowly. Picture that two-handled spoon. If you use it to eat soup, how would you hold its "Y" shape? Would you be able to eat without spilling? Would you hold the handles close to you or on the other side of the bowl?

For a brief moment, your mind was occupied with visualizing something new. It was challenged and it responded. That fraction of a second, where you conceptualize something new—that put you one step closer to the point where good ideas come from. It might sound silly, the idea that thinking of an imaginary spoon can help a person get in touch with the process of innovation, but I challenge you to reflect on what you felt when you imagined it. It wasn't that far away from the feeling you get when you have a useful, innovative idea.

Let's slow down a bit.

I am not saying that thinking of a sculpture of your mind or a two-handled spoon will allow you to finally figure out the problem that has been nagging you for some time. What I am saying is this: that fraction of a second nudged you closer to the process and point from which innovative ideas come.

So, Where Does It Start?

I'd love to tell you where that point is right now, but it is not that easy. That would be like telling you where music comes from. Contemplating the source of music is a surprisingly deep sophism. Would you accept the simple answer that music comes from the instrument? Probably not. How about from the musician? Probably not. How about the mind of the songwriter? How about the mind of the listener?

It's similar to asking where transformative ideas come from. Do transformative ideas come from the brain? From creativity? Where? It's like saying weather comes from the sky. Did you get pleasantly distracted at those sophisms? Good.

Pleasant, relaxed mental states
invite innovation.

PATHWAYS TO GREAT IDEAS

The above exercise is about creating a path, one that allows ideas to arrive more frequently and regularly. If that's too metaphoric, here's the actual foundation on which this exercise and and the entire book is based:

Innovative ideas come from a point and process in your mind developed by regular mental challenges while in an alpha state of consciousness. We use light-hearted sophisms such as the two-handled spoon as envisioning exercises to challenge the mind. These sophisms can put the brain in an alpha state, which is a level of consciousness related to dreaming, daydreams, and being "in the zone."

Relaxation Distraction
Is distracting your consciousness is a way to have innovative ideas appear? When Albert Einstein[4] got stuck on a problem, he stopped thinking about it and played the violin. I'm not saying this process will make you think like Einstein and I'm not saying you should learn the violin. Still, there is a connection between relaxation, mental engagement, and having a good idea.

Cross-Training as a Method of Engagement
Think of this process as cross-training. Swimmers lift weights. Weightlifters run. Runners do yoga. Cross-training prevents injury and also prevents burnout. Constantly thinking about the problem at hand isn't usually effective and can lead to frustration. So, we need to train differently. We need to train our subconscious mind to work with our conscious mind.

Let's Reflect
Will reflecting on the sophisms in this exercise give you an innovative idea right away? Quite possibly, but remember, this process isn't about the short term. No one can get in shape overnight. By regularly stretching and flexing your mind, creativity will flow.

TAKEAWAY FOR THIS WEEK

> Open your notebook. Begin to sketch a model of your mind. If you are not comfortable drawing, continue to mentally shape it, envisioning how you would draw it. Do it when you are relaxed. Set aside a few minutes after your run, before bed, or whenever else you are able to be relaxed enough to let your mind play. This will give your subconscious creative time. I bet you will be amazed at what it delivers.

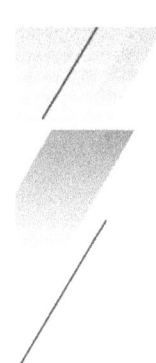

Exercise 3

GATHERING LEGOS

HOW MUCH DO YOU KNOW?

I thought I'd jump right in with something that is fun to think about. Do you know more than Einstein did? How about the President's Chief of Staff, who must keep a zillion details in his head? How about someone with an eidetic memory? (That's a fancy name for a photographic memory.) In order for this exercise to be more meaningful, we must explain the differences between "knowing" and "knowledge."

Defining Knowledge Can Be Tough
If we can't easily define knowledge, how can we say Einstein had any more of it than we do? Did Einstein know your favorite color? Did he know how to order something online? Did he know that sandwiches cut diagonally taste better?

So, is one piece of knowledge more inherently valuable than another? Is the knowledge of fire more important than knowing a pop star's real name? You might say yes, but regarding certain celebrities, just like a wind turbine I'm a huge fan.

What if we said the previous examples aren't real knowledge, that they are simply trivia, unimportant?

GATHERING DIFFERENT TYPES OF KNOWLEDGE

We've touched upon the amount of knowledge.
We've touched upon the value of knowledge.
Let's explore types of knowledge.

YOU KNOW A LOT ABOUT
WHAT YOU KNOW A LOT ABOUT

But what *else* do you know?

How broad is your knowledge? As much as I believe we must know a lot about the area in which we desire a good idea, we should always have knowledge about completely unrelated things. Does this sound like too much work, to gather knowledge about things you're not interested in? I urge you to read Adam Grant's book *Originals*[5]. Grant suggests that innovation comes from mixing knowledge of different domains.

Legos and the Meaning of It All

Let me share a story about my daughter. When my daughter was quite young, she would lose herself for hours in her Lego sets. She was happiest sitting on the floor under her loft bed with countless colored pieces scattered around her. One day, like an over-organized, un-fun psychologist dad who wanted to know what was going on in her mind, I asked her what she was making with her Legos. She was so absorbed that she didn't even look up when she replied, "I don't know, I'm not done yet."

What Does This Have to Do with Helping People Reach Their Professional Goals and Have Revenue-Generating Ideas More Often?

IN A WORD, EVERYTHING

Thoughts and Ideas Come From Knowledge

- New ideas come from assembling accumulated information in new ways.

- New, *innovative ideas* come from assembling information in a new and *useful* way.

This is all done by the subconscious when there are enough knowledge pieces for it to assemble into a new, good idea. Of course, a sales professional should know everything about the product line he is selling, and he should know, in a non-creepy way, everything he can about his clients. But what *else* does he know? Not what *more*. We already know a lot about what we know a lot about. What else does you or your team know?

Let's get back to Legos.

If you only have one set to play with, your creations will be limited and derivative of each other. If you have lots of Lego pieces from different sets, you can create wondrous and weird things that you've never seen before. And just like the many creative things you can make with your Lego sets, the number of ideas you get from different knowledge pieces increases exponentially with the addition of each new piece.

So the more pieces you have...

Get the drift?

So, let's revisit and restate the first question at the beginning of this exercise: how many knowledge pieces do you have? And let's revisit the idea that some ideas might be inherently more valuable than others. Knowing how to tie shoes is more important than knowing that you shouldn't eat a banana from the middle.

More Better Pieces?

Are there some Lego pieces that are *better* than other ones? Maybe. It depends on what you are trying to create. It's the same with knowledge. The knowledge piece of a certain pop star's real name might not be that important unless your client is a huge fan. That specific Lego piece of knowledge might seem unimportant to your conscious mind. But to your subconscious mind, it might be *fascinating*.

Give your subconscious lots of differently colored and shaped pieces to play with. Then give it time play with them. You will be amazed at how it puts your knowledge together in a new way.

TAKEAWAY FOR THIS WEEK

> Just like my daughter showed me, it is tough to have fun and get unstuck if you're only using the same pieces from one Lego set. Using your notebook, make a list of at least five ways that you will gather more Lego pieces. By that I mean gather more knowledge pieces. How? Reading is fantastic, especially if you are reading something outside of your comfort zone. Don't have time to read? What podcasts are you listening to? Are you listening to or reading things about a wide variety of subjects? Reflect on the sophisms in this exercise, then give your subconscious time to assemble an innovative idea. You will be amazed at what it gives you.

Exercise 4

5D PRINTER

Before I begin, let me ask you: when you read the title of this exercise, what did you think? More specifically, what did your subconscious assemble and hand you? Was there a flash of imagination? A wisp of an image of a five-dimensional printer? What did your mental eye see?

Whatever it was, it was the interaction between your subconscious and your conscious mind. That is where innovative ideas are transferred from one place to another, and, as you might know by now, this happens when we are pleasantly distracted. We call that pleasant distraction an alpha state.

If you did not imagine anything, that's ok too Either you were not in a playful alpha state or you did not have enough knowledge pieces about printers or multi-dimensional spacetime. Knowledge pieces? Think of it this way. Your subconscious mind is like a child who is contentedly playing with Lego pieces, snapping them together, taking them apart, and snapping them together in new ways. The Lego pieces represent your accumulated knowledge. (Just in case you skipped it, the previous exercise delves more into knowledge as Lego pieces.)

No Lego Pieces?

What if you don't have the mental Lego piece that represents a 3D printer? What if you have never seen a 3D printer? Then it would be tough for your subconscious mind to put something together to help you imagine a 5D printer. If that's the case, pause right now and quickly pull up a video of a 3D printer. Most of them print with plastic resin, but some print with concrete, and some can even print with protein.[6]

What? Printing Protein?

Think about that next time you don't want to go to the grocery store. I mean, if all food is made up of the same basic building blocks, could we put those building blocks in little compartments in a machine? Then, couldn't they be mixed, injected, and heated to produce any food? That brings us to the psychological concept of structuralism which started with Wilhelm Wundt[7] and was expanded and championed by Edward Titchener.

Structuralism

Structuralism was one of the first approaches to studying the mind. It posits that consciousness, like everything else, is made of smaller structures. The *brain* is made up of neurons, among other things; neurons are made up of even smaller structures. But, what about the *mind* or consciousness? What about *thoughts*? What are thoughts made of?

If we can envision what a thought is made of or looks like, then maybe we can begin to have influence over it. Imagine the benefits of influencing innovative thoughts? At this point, I invite you to go to **Exercise 28 ("Control Room")**. It suggests that those who want to have innovative ideas more frequently envision a control room where you have control of your thoughts, emotions, and body. For instance, what would a relax button look like on your imaginary control panel?

One addition to your control room is going to be a 3D Printer. Just like any printer, it will need ink, toner, or cartridges.

*In case you've skipped the other exercises
and started with this one, a sophism is a pleasant
mental challenge that encourages you to
flex and stretch your mind.*

3D Printer Ink

The first sophism of this exercise asks, what is the ink for a 3D printer of thoughts? What will be the raw materials that are combined and shaped according to the instructions you send it?

Printer Instructions

Our second sophism asks what the instructions are that you send it. What do you want?

What Does This Have to Do with Helping People Reach Their Professional Goals and Have Revenue-Generating Ideas More Often?

TEAMWORK AND THE MATERIAL IT'S MADE OF

Let's extend the metaphor and consider that a well-functioning team or a well-functioning client relationship is like anything that's printed—a letter, sheet music, a three-dimensional model of a new car design. Whatever it may be, it must be made of raw materials. It's not just the people that make up the team, but the relationship between them. What is the raw material that binds them together? For a sales team, what is the raw material that a successful sales relationship is built upon?

Back to Four-Dimension Printing

We know that a three-dimensional printer can use plastic, resin, or even concrete to print an object with width, depth, and height. Those are the three dimensions. So, what is the fourth dimension? Well, before I tell you, please pause to think about that yourself. Consider it our third sophism for this exercise.

Time as the Fourth Dimension

Many physicists agree that the fourth dimension is time. Niel DeGrasse-Tyson describes it by saying that if you were to meet someone, you must have a location that is based on three coordinates and you must meet at a certain time, which is the fourth coordinate or dimension. Without a specified time, you can't meet anyone anywhere.[8]

THE FIFTH DIMENSION

As great as that simple explanation of the fourth dimension is for physics, this is a psychology-based book. So, we're going to go a step beyond. I've always said that if psychology were easy, it would be called any other science. Physics has elaborate equations that, while intricate, still allow universal truths. Unlike physics, psychology doesn't yet have equations and formulas that apply to all people in all situations.

As ethereal, intricate, and even paradoxical as the mind can be, let me suggest for the sake of this book that the mind is the fifth dimension… or at least that the mind is *in* the fifth dimension. That is a fun sophism to play with. If you think that is too broad, let's narrow it. (Can you narrow a dimension?) Let's say that *understanding* is the fifth dimension.

That curiosity you felt at reading that last sentence was probably just like the feeling you had right before your last good idea. By getting into that state more often, you will invite innovative ideas to arrive more often. Remember, increased sales—or whatever business success your goals might be—are only one good idea away.

If we hold the concept of understanding as the fifth dimension (even if just for a short while), then we can ask whether those who understand more or understand better exist more fully in the fifth dimension than those who understand less. Amoebas, for example, can't exist there at all. And, hopefully, you noticed that the previous sentence is soaked in the juices of the fifth dimension because it uses the logical basis of "if…then" statements to help us *understand* the concept of the fifth dimension, which itself made of understanding.

To Be Honest

As I wrote those sentences—or, more specifically, as my fingers typed and as the keyboard encoded the idea of those last sentences—into this document using the raw material of my understanding of the newly printed idea of the fifth dimension, I barely understood what I wrote.

LET'S RECAP

1. The first dimension is **width**.
2. The second is **depth**.
3. The third is height.
4. The fourth is **time**.
5. The fifth is **understanding.**

WHY IS THE FIFTH DIMENSION UNDERSTANDING?

Because it represents a higher level of awareness and knowledge

Notice that understanding happens *after* time. Often ideas develop slowly. This makes a lot of practical sense. If you have ever seen a three-dimensional printer, it is quite slow. If you want another fun sophism, ask yourself how quickly a four-dimensional printer would print time.

Will reflecting on the sophisms in this exercise give you an innovative idea right away? Quite possibly. But this process isn't about the short term. No one can get in shape overnight. By regularly stretching and flexing your mind, creativity will flow.

TAKEAWAY FOR THIS WEEK

> Use your notebook, schedule three times this week when you have a few minutes to think in a pleasantly-relaxed state. No, not the vegetative relaxation of mindless TV watching and not the total involvement of reading a book. Once you find the correct zone, however fleeting it might be, think about any of the sophisms we've discussed. Jot down what comes to mind. Just a few moments of flexing and stretching the mind will help invite your next innovative idea. After you do that, give your subconscious time

You will be impressed by what it brings you.

Exercise 5

DON'T CHASE PUPPIES

Have you ever tried to catch a puppy that didn't want to be caught? Maybe it squeezed through your legs as you held the front door partially open. It's maddening, especially if you need to be somewhere else and the dog simply isn't cooperating with your needs or schedule.

In those situations, the dog doesn't want its play time to end. It loves the game of running away from you so much, it will let you get *just* close enough to give you the false impression that you can get it; when you try, it dashes off again. An astute dog can anticipate any move to catch it and stay one step ahead. There is simply no way for a human to catch a puppy.

Stop Right Now!
Unless…that human stops trying. To the puppy, you chasing it, no matter how frustrating it might be *for you*, is a game. If you stopped chasing it, turned around, and became engaged in something else, that puppy would approach you.

That is a great analogy for engaging with the subconscious and wanting a solution to a problem. Your subconscious, like a playful puppy, doesn't care about your schedule or needs. It wants to play. Chasing it, pressuring it, and trying to get it to do what you want will guarantee that it will run away. Our subconscious (the dog), however, operates on rules that are not only in a different language, but has a completely different grammatical structure and different value system.

What Does This Have to Do with Helping People Reach Their Professional Goals and Have Revenue-Generating Ideas More Often?

We all have bosses. The corporate hierarchy, being what it is, causes sales managers feel downward pressure to meet and beat sales goals. That downward pressure extends to all sales staff.

The Puppy as a Team Metaphor

If you are a sales manager, the question is how hard are you chasing the puppy of your team's improvement. Are you hounding them? (*See what I did there?*) This does not mean a manager should abandon structure and encourage chaos. Sales professionals are at their best when they can explore without having to look over their shoulders. Just like a big sale or an important breakthrough, innovative ideas can't be rushed. You can't demand your subconscious to hurry up and give you a good idea right away any more than you can demand a playful puppy to follow your schedule.

Bye, Bye Puppy

If the puppy represents your subconscious, chasing it will only make it retreat. Why? I don't know. Why might a puppy run away even when you have a treat for it? We could surmise, but we're only guessing. The part of your mind that assembles innovative ideas from raw sensations, your past experiences, and current knowledge follows a value system even more complex than that of a puppy trying to teach a human how to play its game.

Yep, you read that right!

We think puppies should learn what we want. True, but it is also true that they want us to learn what they want. In a thousand different ways, your subconscious wants you to learn how to play with it. That's what this book is about.

So Here's the challenge
If you need a creative solution, take a break from chasing it. Let it come to you. Let your subconscious check on you rather than you continually racking your brain. Make it curious about you. How do we do that?

Invite your mind to play with sophisms.

Here are three:

1. Can a dog understand the idea of tomorrow?

2. How could an expert dog trainer teach a dog the concept of tomorrow?

3. How would your life change if you could smell as well as a puppy?

OPEN MONITORING MEDITATION

Just by taking a brief moment to practice "open monitoring meditation" which is the fancy name for playing with your mind, did your conscious mind take a break from trying to grab the solution before it was ready?[9] If so, you were one step closer to the process and the point from which innovative ideas come. If you want the innovative idea to come to you, stop chasing it so hard. It'll find you. If it hasn't found you yet, don't go chasing it; give it a reason to come to you.

To help, play with this sophism:

What does your subconscious want?

TAKEAWAY FOR THIS WEEK

> **Don't find time. Make time.** Make time for yourself. More specifically, make time to think about your subconscious. Once you have a time and a place, sit quietly, relax, and breathe for a few minutes. Ask yourself what would make your subconscious want to play with you, to bring you a good idea? Reflect on the sophisms in this exercise. Write down your reflections and answers. Then, give your subconscious time to assemble an innovative idea.

You will be amazed at what it gives you.

Exercise 6:

HOW MANY NUMBERS ARE THERE?

There are three kinds of people in the world: those who can count and those who can't.

Did you just have a mental stutter step? If so, that amusement and relaxation you felt was just like the feeling you had right before your last good idea. By getting into that state more often, you will invite innovative ideas to arrive more often. Remember, increased sales—or whatever your goals might be—are only one good idea away.

And by the way…were you wondering what the third kind of people are?

Infinite Divisibility

Let's take a look at an intriguing math concept—infinity—and how it can be used to develop creative flexibility. To start, a seemingly simple question: how many numbers are between 1 and 2? Between 1 and ½?

Did you do another mental stutter step? I bet, after a brief moment when your subconscious popped its head up and wanted to play, your conscious mind came up with the answer—

Infinite

Infinite really isn't an answer. It is an ill-defined concept. Take a minute and picture a ruler. Mentally envision a small part of it, between 1 and 2. Then between 1 and ½. Imagine all of the hash marks between 1 and ½. How many are there? Go deeper. Imagine the space between two hash marks. Now go deeper. Divide that into 10 segments. Got it? Now, pick two of them and go deeper. Divide the space between those into 10 segments.

Not only is that a great mental exercise for you (and me) to do when we are relaxed, it is a good metaphor for this exercise.

THE INFINITE RULER AND MENTAL EXERCISE

Before we get to the metaphor, let's talk about the mental exercise part of the infinite ruler. When you envisioned the ruler, what *color* was it? Did you *consciously* choose the color of the ruler? Probably not. Yet, the picture of the ruler came from somewhere. Your subconscious.

Microcosmic Interpretation

Notice how cool that is. You didn't choose what it would look like, your subconscious did. You were not consciously focused on the look of the ruler. That is a micro example of what we are hoping to do with the Creativity Algorithm:

Distract the conscious mind so the subconscious mind can deliver innovative ideas.

Infinite Solutions

Now, onto the metaphor. Well, maybe not a metaphor; just a hopeful connection between two concepts.

> *If there are actually an infinite number of numbers within what is commonly thought of as a very small interval, then there must be an infinite number of solutions to any given problem.*

Is that a huge leap? Often when people are mentally stuck, they think there are no options. In my talks, classes, and other parts of my life, I have mentioned this "infinite solutions" concept to people who are stuck. Quite frankly, they get upset because it seems like I am minimizing their problems. That is the last thing I want to do, because when people get upset or defensive, then getting into an alpha state or flow state where your subconscious mind wants to play becomes substantially harder.

Impossibilities

Worse and weirdly, when people become defensive, they often defend the thing that is preventing growth. That defensiveness then becomes a distraction from finding the solution. It isn't hard to imagine a stressed sales manager who feels backed into a corner. In order to salvage some emotional value, he must hold onto the idea that his situation is impossible. Because if it weren't impossible, then he, an expert in his business, would have found the solution by now.

If I were to suggest to him that there are an infinite number of solutions to the problem he is facing, he would dig in further with his argument that the solution is impossible. To avoid blame that only exists in his mind, he would reject me as an outsider who doesn't know his business.

What Does This Have to Do with Helping People Reach Their Professional Goals and Have Revenue-Generating Ideas More Often?

Let's imagine a situation where a sales professional is stuck, either in their professional life or personal life. How can that salesperson's manager avoid minimizing the problem? Even more challenging, how can such a manager resist the urge to simply step in and solve the problem? Other people's solutions might be fine, but they are rarely as satisfying as solutions that we come up with ourselves. So, a better question is how can a manager lead his employee to the solution that can surely be assembled by the employee's mind.

Zeno's Paradox

Let's go back to that ruler that some readers may recognize as a version of Zeno's Paradox[1]. The number of times a ruler can be divided is infinite. You know what else is infinite? The human imagination. How am I so sure? In the nearly 200,000 years that billions of humans have been on Earth, no one has found the limit to our imagination.

For those who are skeptical, try this sophism.

> *Try to find the limit, if not of humankind's imagination, then of yours.*

Sophistic Parent

If you wanted a sophism, that is the mother of all sophisms:

> *Find the limit of your imagination.*

What if you could map all of the possible combinations of thoughts that your subconscious could put together? What if the imaginary sales manager from a few paragraphs ago mapped his subconscious? Would he find the solution that he swears is impossible?

Right Place, Wrong Way

If you have read the previous exercises, you know the sales manager isn't looking in the wrong *place*, he is looking in the wrong *way*. In fact, maybe he should stop looking altogether. Just like it is difficult to purposely relax, it is difficult to purposely be creative.

As we know, stress is the antithesis of creativity.

TAKEAWAY FOR THIS WEEK

> Grab your notebook, jot down the details of the ruler that popped into your mind. Work on the imaginary ruler. Go deeper. How many levels can you get to? Write that down. Try again. Write that down too. And here is the cool part: when you get distracted and stop concentrating on it, that is your subconscious wanting to play. Get distracted. It's good for you. Just don't *try* to get distracted. Just a few moments of flexing and stretching the mind will help invite your next innovative idea. After you do that, give your subconscious time; you will be impressed by what it brings you.

Exercise 7

AFTERTHOUGHTS

"Afterthoughts" is a word that's usually used following an event. In my mind, afterthoughts are usually tinged with regret.

First Sophism:

Can unshared, unacted-on ideas cause regret?

As we discussed in the "**Gathering Legos**" **exercise (Exercise 3)**, the subconscious mind, like children playing with Legos, assembles innovative ideas when the conscious mind is pleasantly distracted. What does it assemble them from? **Raw materials**.

Those raw materials are

1. knowledge

2. experience

3. regrets.

If you have ever played with Legos, let me ask you this. Are there any bad Lego pieces? Bad colors? Bad shapes? Boring shapes? I'm going to say no. Each and every Lego piece can be assembled into *something*. What if I said there was no bad knowledge? Or bad experiences? (Note: I am not trivializing anyone's trauma or pain; this is merely a thought exercise.)

What Does This Have to Do with Helping People Reach Their Professional Goals and Have Revenue-Generating Ideas More Often?

SILOING AND AI

Think about hiring someone. Often, we think of highly qualified people as siloed[2]. They are very deep and very tall in one specific field. That is fantastic if you only want them to do one thing. But if that one thing is so routine, then it can be done—and will likely eventually be done—by AI.

We hire people for their minds. Deep knowledge is important, but it can be taught on the job. Broad knowledge, however, is based on experience. Broad experience can't easily be taught on the job. Next time you hire someone, take a look at their metaphorical Lego collection. Is it a lot of the same type of pieces with the same colors, or is it a hodgepodge of all types of pieces?

With regard to the Creativity Algorithm, we are generally concerned with things that can't be measured easily. Psychologists have tried. Boy, how they have tried! [3]There are tons of purported creativity tests. There are even some that have the backing of major corporations and brands.

But that's like measuring nature by what appears in your backyard. Sure, there can be lots of species and different weather, but the constraints and limited scope of your backyard make it an unscientific way of studying nature in general. Similarly, the constraints of a specific creativity test make it an baseless way to study creativity.

Where Do Thoughts Go?
OK, so we eschew attempts to make creativity tangible, even though the name of this book is "The Creativity Algorithm." If we don't want to nail down creativity and stretch it out on a dissection table, what is the point of this exercise? Well, let's think about the title.

Missing Thoughts
Where do your thoughts go after you've had them? That's a heck of a sophism. If that's too esoteric, then think of something concrete. Think of your phone number right now. Seriously, recall it from something called your preconscious. Got it? All ten digits?

Now I am going to distract you with a horrible joke. Ready?

> **Two atoms were walking down the street.**
> **One said, "Oh Darn, I lost an electron."**
> **The other said, "Are you sure?"**
> **The first one said, "Yeah, I'm positive."**

While that is a classically awful dad joke, my main concern is where did your phone number go when you were reading and processing the joke?

That amusement and relaxation you felt wondering where your phone number went was just like the feeling you had right before your last good idea. By getting into that state more often, you will invite innovative ideas to also arrive more often.

Remember,

*Increased sales—or whatever your goals might be—
are only one good idea away.*

Back to Legos

Did the version of the phone number go back into the pile of Legos, which is a spot on metaphor for the accumulated knowledge of your life? Did it simply vanish like steam on a cold day? If it vanished, isn't that wasteful? Each time you think of your phone number are you using raw material and then just throwing it away? Do you have an inexhaustible amount of raw material for making thoughts?

Waste Not

Does that mean that the relaxation exercises that lead us to an alpha state are a waste? (If this is your first exercise, an alpha state is a type of relaxation that has a person's mind pleasantly active. Sometimes known as being "in the zone," it is the mental state that allows the subconscious to deliver transformative ideas to the conscious mind.)

We can't count thoughts before they happen. Even the mind must follow the rules of time. As discussed in **Exercise 4 ("5D Printer")**, the fourth dimension is time and the fifth dimension is understanding. Yet understanding must happen within a certain time, right?

*Can you understand something before
the thought is formed?*

That is a great sophism to ponder.

It would be much easier to count thoughts *after* they happen, but thoughts don't continue to exist if we are not thinking of them. Or do they? Is a memory just a blurry snapshot of the dissipating smoke cloud of a thought? Is counting memories the same as counting thoughts?

TAKEAWAY FOR THIS WEEK

Imagine a factory smokestack. After a point, we can't see the smoke as it dissipates into the atmosphere. As soon as our gaze follows it to where it cannot be seen, we readjust our gaze to the top of the stack to look at the densest part of the smoke cloud and follow it upward. Is that like our consciousness? As soon as we are done with a thought, do we readjust our awareness to where our consciousness is most dense? Let's keep going with this. If the smoke cloud is a thought, and the factory is the subconscious, what is the raw material that the factory burns to make the cloud? Using your notebook, draw a smokestack. Push yourself to envision, then label what the mental smoke is make of.

Exercise 8

THE POINT OF RELAXING

Cartridges? X-Men? What?
Have you ever played an old video game, the kind that required cartridges? Way back in the day, I played a video game at a friend of a friend's house. It was the early '90's so the resolution and graphics were pitiful by today's standards. The game was based on the Marvel Comics heroes, the X-Men. Despite it being so long ago, one thing about that game has stuck with me.

The game was similar to many other action-based video games. You would choose a character who had certain advantages and disadvantages and use that character to jump, punch, and kick their way through the bad guys of the game. Of course, whichever character was played, they, too, would get punched and kicked by the bad guys. If you've ever played those games, you know that there is a little health meter in the corner of the screen that shows declining health of the character each time they get kicked or punched by the bad guys.

One of the characters in that X-Men game was "Wolverine." Like the other characters, when he got punched, kicked, or shot with a laser beam by the aforementioned bad guys, his little health meter at the top right of the screen would decrease with each blow he absorbed. But, unlike the other characters, Wolverine could heal. If left alone in a safe spot in the game, his health meter would slowly fill back up. Basically, if he relaxed, he could rejuvenate.

What Does This Have to Do with Helping People Reach Their Professional Goals and Have Revenue-Generating Ideas More Often?

Is the resting of a fictional 2-dimensional character the same as our efforts to relax. Do we simply take a few minutes of not doing anything just so after those few minutes, we can do even more work? They take a few minutes of not doing anything, so that after those few minutes, they can do *even more* things.

More is Less or??

That leads us to the purpose of relaxing. I think you can already see where this is going. Relaxation shouldn't be just a tool for production. We shouldn't relax simply so we can do more work. We should relax because the process itself is valuable, not just because of the product we hope to obtain.

> Let me summarize a story.
>
> > Two employees were talking with each other in that water-cooler way that employees do.
> >
> > One person said, "There needs to be another day in the week."
> >
> > The second person asked, "Oh yeah? What would you do with an eighth day?"
> >
> > The first person replied, "I would catch up on my work."
>
> That's an interesting take on a day off. I suggest that relaxation has its own point and that that point is not just so we can rest and start working again. Similarly, I worry that if we rest *only* to get innovative ideas, we'll

get neither rest nor get innovative ideas. We should rest to rest.

What's the Point?
OK, all of that sounds reasonable. Rest for rest's sake. Yadda, yadda. We completely missed the point of the question of this exercise's title. We assumed *point* meant *purpose*.

Location, Location, Location
Let's think of point like a location, something like the point on a map. What is the point of relaxing? *Where* does it happen? If you immediately answer in your hammock or on the beachthat's 100% fine. Those are great *physical* locations.

Where does relaxation happen mentally? Did you think of an ethereal cloud-like location in your mind, as if your mind is a place. Does relaxation happen when you stop thinking? But that last sentence has the word *when*. This exercise is about examining *where* relaxation happens in your mind.

Stop reading. Take a second or two. Play with this sophism.

Where does creativity happen?

For a brief moment, did you have a map of your mind? Did you think of a room in your house? Is that visualization of relaxation coming from a *point* in your mind? (Remember, we can't be 100% sure the mind actually exists. But that's a discussion for a future exercise.)

Relaxation Is Tricky
Whatever you thought of, notice that you were not thinking of the problem for which you needed a solution. That sophism gave and still gives your mind the ability to relax. Notice the phrasing of that sentence: your *mind* was relaxed; but were *you*? Relaxation is a tricky thing. It's like the puppy metaphor—the more you chase it, the less likely you'll catch (obtain) it. Go back a few minutes and remember what you felt and what you saw when you pictured the point of relaxation. Just pause and bring it to

the front of your mind. Whatever you imagine brings you one step closer to the point and process from which innovative ideas come.

Remember that the core idea of the Creativity Algorithm is mentally, manipulating cognitive puzzles called sophisms. While in a relaxed state that will create an inviting environment for innovative ideas to arrive.

Will reflecting on sophisms give you an innovative idea right away? Maybe. Remember, this process isn't about the short term. No one can get in shape overnight. By regularly stretching and flexing your mind, creativity will flow.

TAKEAWAY FOR THIS WEEK

> I think you should dive back into contemplating the point of relaxation. Is it between other points? Is it a point by itself, or is it near other points? Before you do that, take some time to get into a relaxed alpha state that we discussed in the first exercise. There are many ways to get into an alpha state, so do what works best for you, but make an effort to sit and physically relax. Then slip into your mind. Then look for the point of relaxation. After you relax and search for the point of relaxation, jot down what you thought about. Doing so will make your thoughts more real.

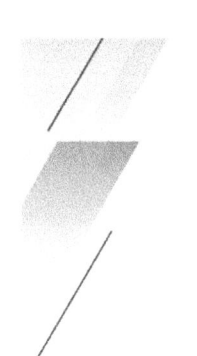

Exercise 9

DEFINING CREATIVITY

Let me start with a little story. Years ago, there was a huge traffic jam. It seemed that a truck driver forgot how tall his trailer was and drove under a bridge. Fortunately, he wasn't going very fast. After a horrendous shrieking noise, the truck came to a shuddering stop. It seemed the driver was going just fast enough and the trailer was just high enough that it wedged itself under the bridge. The bridge didn't suffer much from the impact and the trailer wasn't horribly damaged. But it was stuck. Authorities arrived on the scene quickly. They worried if they used the truck's power to pull the trailer through, it would damage the bridge or the truck.

State police, local police, highway administrators, and civil engineers were milling about, shaking their heads, and doing their best to figure out how to get the truck out of there. While they were puzzling this out, the traffic jam just kept getting longer and longer. Maybe they could grease the top of the trailer? Maybe they could bring in a crane to lift the bridge an inch. Bridges are designed to expand and contract, right? The most expensive idea was to cut out a section of the bridge, drive the truck out, then repair the bridge. Each professional was stuck in a so-called "mental set" that was defined by the nature of their jobs.[4]

After a certain amount of time, a young boy approached the frazzled experts and simply suggested that they let some air out of the truck's tires.

What Does This Have to Do with Helping People Reach Their Professional Goals and Have Revenue-Generating Ideas More Often?

STUCK

When a sales professional is trying to find a way to get sales moving again—just like when the engineers were trying to get the truck moving again—they are often stuck in a mental set of what has worked in the past. Or, even worse, they are stuck in a mental set of thinking only from their point of view.

*We should all seek solutions from
a wide range of sources.*

Defining Creativity
Trying to find a solution to a problem by only thinking about what worked in the past is a great way to *not* find that solution. By definition, limiting our thinking prevents creativity. Was the little boy creative? Before we answer, we must define our terms. That previous sentence can and should be said before every research question.

There is not a unified, agreed-upon definition of creativity. And that probably doesn't surprise you. Creativity is a subset of intelligence, and, as I'm sure you know, that is a very tough concept to define. Like other things in psychology, trying to define intelligence or creativity has been described as trying to nail jelly to a wall.

Despite it being a difficult concept to define, that doesn't mean we shouldn't try. Increasing sales might be difficult, but—well, I don't have to finish that thought.

Can Creativity Be Defined?

Let's pause here. If you have read the previous exercises, you probably know what is coming next: a sophism. How can we define something that doesn't exist? I'll repeat it, in case you read that last sentence too fast.

How can we define something that doesn't exist?

Prove It!

I'd like you to take a minute and try to prove creativity exists? If you can't do it right now as you read, then try it later today or tomorrow after you have let yourself enter an alpha state. In fact, I think you should make time in your calendar to do it. 15 minutes. Ten minutes to relax and five minutes to ponder how you can prove creativity exists.

Notice that I didn't say to give an example of it. I said to prove that it exists. Giving an example is relatively easy. But we are not about easy cognitive tasks, just like we aren't about easy sales tasks. Later today or tomorrow, sit down, enter an alpha state (even if you are not good at it yet, it is a good idea to practice), and find a way to prove creativity exists.

Do you see what I did there? I asked you to keep your mind busy by proving creativity exists. It might be a simple cognitive trick, but trying not to think of something like an example of creativity in sales is one of the surest ways to have it pop into your mind. So, keep thinking about how to prove creativity exists. Don't know how to get started? Imagine that you are a trial lawyer. What evidence would you bring? Who is your opposing counsel? Who is on the jury?

Define It!

Let's keep going with our effort to prove creativity exists. In order to prove it exists, you must define it. The root word of *definition* is *fin*, which means an end or limit. Can we put a box around the concept of creativity? Can we limit where it starts and ends? Does your definition leave certain things out? Often by trying to achieve a goal, we are told to focus on one step at a time. Remember: in the key question, I didn't ask you to just define it; I asked you to go beyond that step and prove that it exists.

Skip It!

Every engineer in the world might throw a fit at the notion of skipping a step. I can almost hear safety inspectors and quality control experts gasp at the mere mention. But your subconscious doesn't care about procedure and protocols. It operates according to rules we cannot fathom, because, by definition, we are unconscious of them. By relaxing and not chasing the solution to an implied problem, the solution is more likely to appear.

Being in an alpha state while you ponder a sophism will not guarantee a good idea. Rather it will invite your subconscious to think without the constraints of a specific mental set.

TAKEAWAY FOR THIS WEEK

> Do your best to prove creativity exists. If it helps, write down the evidence you have that will prove the point, just as a lawyer might prepare his case. Before you try, allow yourself to get into an alpha state. Then concentrate on proving creativity exists. Do that consciously with focus. Be the engineers who were concentrating on getting the truck out. Maybe, just maybe, your subconscious might bring you a definition of creativity. Or, better yet, it might just roll up on a bicycle and bring the proof that creativity exists in the form of the solution you've been looking for.

Exercise 10

ACADEMIC DEFINITION

Money Isn't Everything, Is It?

Have you ever taken a philosophy class? Many people find them frustrating. It seems like students pay a lot of tuition for a class that will introduce seemingly impossible questions such as how to figure out what is the higher good? That sophism is an oldie and a goodie. Expensive tuition does not guarantee that students will leave with satisfactory answers.

Creativity is much the same. And that shouldn't surprise us. I don't think the problem rests with the complexity of the subject, even though the subject is as difficult to study as dreams are hard to interpret. Creativity can't be seen under a microscope, telescope, or any other measuring device. Even if we did have a tool to "see" it, that tool would be subject to quite a few variables, just like the variables of trying to figure out what is right or wrong.

I also don't think the problem rests with researchers and theoreticians. They apply proper scientific methods to study creativity. Science moves slowly. Accumulating scientific knowledge is akin to watching single grains of sand fall through a narrow opening. Each study adds one more grain onto the pile of human knowledge.

Categorize It?
What if I said the problem with having an agreed upon idea of creativity rests in the very thing trying to do the defining—the human mind. Relatedly, stop categorizing this as a *problem*. The human mind loves to categorize things. In fact, it is difficult *not* to categorize things.

Here's another sophism: try to find one thing that cannot be categorized. Wanting to categorize creativity as not a *problem*, but an *opportunity* is, in fact, our predilection for categorizing things. That might be the very tool we need to study creativity.

Mind Laundry
For example, imagine you are cleaning up a bedroom. What's the first thing you do? Separate clean clothes and dirty clothes? When you have all the dirty clothes, what do you do? Categorize them into different colors and fabrics for different laundry loads

To Sit or Not to Sit
Consider a chair. If the back is removed, does it become a stool? Now consider a stool. If you add arm rests, does it become a chair? It is a fun sophism to think on: what is the precise characteristic of "chair-ness" that makes something a chair?

Categorical Options
Does that mean you can't think of anything that cannot be put into a category? Play with that sophism. I wouldn't be surprised if thinking about the questions in this paragraph allowed you to slip into an alpha state. If those questions distracted you, then you were in a similar state to the one you were in when you had your last good idea.

CHARACTERIZING CREATIVITY

Despite the ethereal nature of it, there are two generally agreed-upon components of creativity—originality/newness and utility/appropriateness.[5]

Originality/Newness

Originality seems fairly self-explanatory. However, it has quite a few layers and nuances. Think of a portable and miniature drying rack for a just-washed dish. Just one dish. The rack is a curved piece of metal that allows a plate to sit almost flat, but not quite flat, on a counter. Airflow can get under it. Best of all, it wasn't necessary to invent, make, or forge anything. Simply take a spoon out of your silverware drawer and set a wet plate on it.

*Does that meet the criteria of originality?
A spoon on a counter?*

Let's Be Clear

We can further categorize originality by looking at whether it is simply new to the person who thought of it or whether it is new to humankind. Consider that nearly every day, countless children discover something that is new to them but that has been known to billions of others.

Utility/Appropriatness

Utility might be an even squishier concept to try to fit into a nice, tidy category. There are plenty of things that exist that are of questionable utility. Think of a staff meeting. Isn't its utility completely subjective?

A spoon as drying rack might be just the thing for a particular person at a particular moment in time, but it is hardly useful on a large scale. Now, consider a water desalination machine. Taking the salt out of ocean water to irrigate crops could provide food for billions. But such a machine needs a fusion reactor because of the power demands. Fusion reactors do not exist yet. So how useful is a machine that cannot be turned on?

Paperweights?

Perhaps we can think of creativity as the intersection between something original and something useful. A two-handled spoon (from Exercise 1, "Introduction to the Creativity Algorithm") or a flat bowl might be new, but not useful. A new rock might be useful as a paperweight, but even though *you* recently dug it up, it isn't actually an original idea.

What Does This Have to Do with Helping People Reach Their Professional Goals and Have Revenue-Generating Ideas More Often?

Often, management forgets the little things that can have a compounding effect. An employee might be one thought away from a huge, multi-million-dollar idea. But maybe something is preventing him or her from having that transformative idea. Maybe expectations should be reset and we should start with something of a more narrow utility. Maybe start with something that has high utility to a narrow group of employees. If you are a manager, encourage your employees to start by making *their job* easier, better, and more efficient, then see what happens. It is likely that the gains in efficiency from that one employee's idea about improving their job will snowball into gains for the whole organization.

TAKEAWAY FOR THIS WEEK

Pick a time to pick a process. A relaxation process. Maybe it is the same one you are used to. If it works, great; stick with it. In later exercises, we'll work on different methods of relaxation. Once you are relaxed, do not think of a useful solution to something at work. Instead, reflect on whether everything must have a category. Using your notebook jot down whatever comes to mind. Then reflect on whether your subconscious brought "you" ideas from the same category or whether it brought "you" ideas of different categories. Will reflecting on this sophism or any sophism deliver you a good idea? It's likely. The important ingredient is trust. Trust your subconscious, give it time, and welcome the idea.

Exercise 11

PLANT ANOTHER GARDEN

As Ye Sew

I am a terrible gardener. The time and money I have wasted could have easily seeded (see what I did there) a different hobby that I might have actually enjoyed. No matter how bad I am now, I was even worse in previous years. In fact, I might have been the world's worst gardener. You might ask, where is your evidence? But that's just it. I don't have any. Nothing grew. No matter how much I tried, I couldn't get things to grow which is a great metaphor for a professional who feels stuck.

I tried everything. I'd water. Fertilize. Prune. Weed. Water more. Fertilize more. Prune stuff that didn't need pruning and so on. I would check on my plants and grass frequently. Several times per day. Nothing I did made things grow faster. In retrospect, I am sure that I over-watered, over-fertilized, and generally overdid it. My efforts were preventing the natural growth of the plants.

What Does This Have to Do with Helping People Reach Their Professional Goals and Have Revenue-Generating Ideas More Often?

Don't Overdo It

Getting the best out of your people is like getting the best yield from a plant. Over watering it, over fertilizing it, and general fiddling doesn't help it produce vegetables. I'm not saying managers should leave their people alone. Bean plants need something to climb on and the most productive tomato plant needs a cage for support *(see Exercise 33, "Tomato Cage")*.

I think this might ring true for many of us when it comes to dealing with our subconscious. Previously, we have used the metaphor of a puppy to represent the subconscious part(s) of our mind that offer(s) us solutions. (Notice that I put the "s" within parentheses. I don't know if there is more than one subconscious part of our mind that playfully delivers ideas to us.) Wouldn't that be something? To have several?

That's a good sophism:

Are there different types of the subconscious that deliver different types of innovative ideas?

Ponder?

Will pondering whether there are different parts of your subconscious give you an innovative idea right away? Maybe, but this process isn't about the short term. No one can get in shape overnight. By regularly stretching and flexing your mind, creativity will flow.

Racking Your Brain

You might have heard the phrase "racking your brains," sometimes spelled as "wracking your brain." To rack means to cause emotional torment, while to wrack means to cause physical damage. Either way, it refers to causing stress and trauma. As such, racking or wracking to find a solution to a problem or trying to make a good idea come to you is like constantly fiddling with the fragile shoots in a garden or walking on the very grass you're trying to grow. You're expending a lot of effort towards what will likely be a null outcome.

Looking Back

What if I planted the seed, made sure the soil is fertile, watered it, and left it alone? In retrospect, that is what I should have done. That's the same with problem solving. Wracking your brain will not make the solution grow any faster.

The Necessity of Letting Grow

We humbly must remember that many things do not *care* about or even *know about* our schedules. Plants, puppies, and the subconscious are blissfully unaware of our plans and deadlines.

May I Suggest

Let your subconscious do what it wants to do on its own timeline. Even if you could rush it to produce ideas more quickly, would you be getting the best ideas? Should you pick a vegetable before it's ready?

Easy for me to tell you thatd, to just sit there and watch your garden grow. If you are reading this, you probably have several to-do lists and you might be managing other people's to-do lists as well. You can't just sit, do nothing, and *wait* for a money-making idea.

Can You Really Just Sit and Wait?

Plant Different

Instead of doing nothing while you wait, how about planting *another* garden? Till up the soil. Get your hands dirty with something *else*. Plant a seed. Give it what it needs and leave it alone. How long will that new project take you? Long enough for the first garden to sneakily produce something when you aren't looking.

Pillars of Creativity and Growth

The growing and incubation periods are important for creativity for many reasons. The easiest analogy to make is comparing your mind to a muscle. Even well-trained muscles need rest. I suggest that if you are reading this, your conscious mind is well-trained. It is organized, task-oriented, and focused. But, no matter how good you are at problem-solving; your mind needs breaks.

That means we have two things to do for this exercise.

1. Take a break from the problem at hand.

2. Find a new challenge.

That isn't always easy because the mind and the body like their routines. They resist change and newness. However, change and newness are the pillars of creativity.[6]

Before you try to find that new puzzle or hobby online, take three deep breaths and focus on the exhales. How do they feel? If you don't have a word for how they feel, take three more breaths and try again. Concentrate on describing the breaths. If you really concentrated on the breaths, you probably noticed how you were *not* thinking of anything else. In effect, you were planting a different garden while your subconscious mind was still working on the task you were doing before you did the first three breaths.

New Idea, New Revenue?

You want to think of a money-making idea? That's fine, but the most direct way to do that is to think of a hobby you haven't started yet. Or think of the hobby that you once enjoyed and would like to restart. The subconscious mind doesn't often follow straight lines.

If relaxing is tilling up the soil in our mental garden, then thinking of the hobby is planting the seed. Making enjoyable time to engage in your hobby is the fertilizer. I suggest if making the time becomes another stressor, then maybe now is not the time for that garden.

Just as you can't force something to grow in a garden, you can't make yourself grow and develop new techniques if you're too stressed about making time for yet another thing. If you can't find the time to work on that hobby, puzzle, garden, etc., leave it alone. You planted the seeds. Go try a different one.

Concentration Limitation

In a later exercise we'll go into detail to prove that the human mind cannot *consciously* concentrate on more than one thing at a time. But that fact isn't true for the subconscious. Your subconscious can multitask in literally unnacountable number of ways. If you're struggling for a solution or looking for a good idea, take your conscious mind off the problem. Let your subconscious handle it. Don't worry; it can...

As long as you give it time.

Don't OverGarden It

For sales managers, what if we define your employees as the seeds or plants? Are you constantly digging, fertilizing, pruning, and otherwise bothering the garden? What if you allow them to grow and their ideas to incubate? What if instead of constantly managing them, you go start a new garden?

TAKEAWAY FOR THIS WEEK

> Take ten deep inhales. For this week, concentrate on the inhalation part of the breath. In later exercises, we'll explore different ways to inhale. For this week, pick two sessions where you can witness yourself inhale 10 times. Then do not try to think of a solution. Rather, try to think of a new puzzle. Write down three minor problems that you can work on while your subconscious assembles the solution to a different problem.

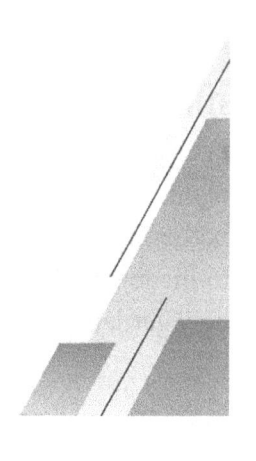

Exercise 12

WHAT COMES FIRST?

If you were to make a list of the most common things in all schools, of all levels, I bet multiple-choice tests would be near the top. Not all schools have lockers and not all schools have chalk boards, but I bet all schools use multiple-choice.

A, B, C, D

Multiple-choice tests attempt to simplify and categorize what is happening in a mind into four or more choices. The idea that we can simplify the internal workings of the mind is seductive. That is the allure of multiple-choice or any other psychometric test. Can the mind or its parts be measured and categorized like a multiple-choice test or chemistry's periodic table of elements?

That is a pretty good sophism. Even better is the question of whether such a table of mental elements would be the same for each person's mind.

WHAT COMES FIRST?

Neural Thinking Confusion?
In my psychology class, a recurring question comes up:

Does thinking cause neural activity or does neural activity cause thoughts?

I'm defining Neural activity here as the tiny electrical charges produced by neurons as they chemically communicate with other neurons.[7]

Thinking The Body Electric
So, the question is, when you had a good idea in the past, did measurable, physical neural activity cause the *im*measurable, ethereal thought to appear? Or, did the coalescing thought cause an uncountable number of neurons to make electricity? That is another good sophism.

As mentioned above, having a good idea is almost always pleasant. Moreover, pondering sophisms such as the ones found in these exercises is also pleasant. So, does a pleasant state of mind allow for deeper pondering of sophisms? Or does pondering sophisms allow for a pleasant state of mind? That's another cool sophism.

All work and no play
As you might have noticed from earlier exercises, I encourage readers to make some time for themselves to relax and stretch their minds with sophisms. But what if you just can't relax? What if the concerns of the real world and your to-do lists just will not let go of you? Well, then try it backward. Don't try to relax and then play with sophisms. Play with the sophisms and see if relaxation will come to you. Counterintuitively, doing will lead to relaxing.

Here are some thoughts to distract and engage. The intersection of distraction and engagement is where innovative ideas come from.

- Can psychology create a table of elements that is universal for each mind?

- Does chemical/electrical activity cause innovative ideas, or, rather, do innovative ideas cause chemical/electrical activity?

- Do pleasant thoughts allow for relaxation, or, rather, does relaxation cause pleasant thoughts?

In a future exercise, we'll experiment with this. We will use your smartwatch to measure heartbeats per minute. We'll get a "before-thinking-of-a-sophism number" and an "after-thinking-of-a-sophism number." Overtly, we will be measuring heart rate, but will we also be measuring relaxation?

What Does This Have to Do with Helping People Reach Their Professional Goals and Have Revenue-Generating Ideas More Often?

Quota Then, Quota Now

Do previous years' sales numbers drive the next year's quota structure, or does the quota structure drive the sales numbers? Do happy, productive employees allow managers to be great or do great managers set the conditions that allow employees to be happy and productive.

Management Professionals, this is where I will ask you to come up with your own what-came-first sophism. Can you think of a situation or relationship where you are not sure what comes first? Seeking uncertainty might seem counterintuitive, especially to organizations that have defined structures and protocols. But uncertainty is where opportunity lies.

Linear, hierarchical thinking does not encourage creativity.

Sales professionals, do your clients like you because you've solved their problems or do they let you solve their problems because they like you?

Let's Think About This
Will reflecting on circular logic within your profession lead you to more frequent money-making ideas? Maybe, but again, it is the process of keeping your conscious mind distracted with circular logic that will allow your subconscious to deliver a good idea.

Conscious-Subconscious
The conscious goal of thinking of a what-comes-first relationship within your profession, is that you will find something that can be explored and improved.

The subconscious goal is that while you are consciously thinking of your organizational processes, your subconscious might just sneak up on you with an amazing idea. Not sure thinking about those processes will invite your subconscious to play?

Try this circular sophism,

if a snake named Ouroboros started eating its tail, got to its stomach and ate it, where would it go if the snake swallowed it?

TAKEAWAY FOR THIS WEEK

> Don't relax first. Put a note in your calendar to find 10 minutes in the middle of your workday. Set a timer for 10 minutes. Note your stress level on scale from 1 to 10. Write down the number. Then challenge your mind with one of the above sophisms for 10 minutes. If you veer off topic and begin to think of your to-do list, that's OK. Gently guide yourself back to the sophism. When the 10-minute alarm goes off, note your stress level. Write it down. As always, play with these sophisms, and then give your subconscious time to assemble a good idea. Not only will you be surprised by what it delivers to you, you will be surprised by when it delivers it to you.

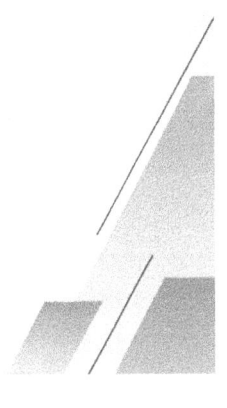

Exercise 13

BIG C AND LITTLE C

Big-C ideas are innovative ideas that have a big effect on lots of people.[8] On the other side, we have Little-"c" ideas that are found in things like life hack videos. Big-"C" ideas are things like the internet, Coltrane's jazz, and the Theory of Relativity. That's not to say that Little-"c" ideas are unimportant or aren't beneficial[9]. They simply don't have a big impact on lots of people.

Do you worry about wasting time? Most people do. As I'm typing this, I feel like I am falling behind on my to-do list.

The problem I have is that the place where I do my work—my laptop—is also the same place where I can waste hours. Maybe I'll just veer off topic and talk about veering off topic.

So Let's Veer!

I think my worst enemy is those click-bait videos on "life hacks." They are short clips that show us how we have been using products wrong or doing things the hardest way possible. I like those videos so much that I actually bookmark them as though I were a hoarder of good ideas. I collect the videos and the ideas they contain just in case I happen to spill a one-pound bag of flour on my car's carpet, and I need an easy way to get the flour out of the carpet using only a coat hanger, a bale of hay, and a snorkel. OK, I might have veered off there more than just a bit, but still, I love those types of videos.

Most importantly, if you have been reading to this point, you might begin to wonder where I'm going with this. I don't think of watching those videos as wasting time. I think they reflect my brain regulating itself.

$E=CT^2$

Consciously thinking is expensive in terms of the body's energy demand[10]. The brain is responsible for consuming 20% of the oxygen of the body. The prefrontal cortex of the frontal lobe is the part of the brain that is commonly associated with concentration. That part of the brain gets tired easily[11].

Thus and Thereby

So, let's get back to the point of veering off from the main point. I love life-hack videos and because website algorithms track our every click, they know that I love life-hack videos. Thus, I am fed a steady stream of those videos whenever I need a brain break, and, of course, I watch them, strengthening the algorithm and perpetuating the cycle.,

I am lucky enough to be able to let myself be distracted for only a few moments, maybe just long enough for my prefrontal cortex to catch its breath and be passive instead of active. (I hope that that last sentence reads as a nod of understanding and support to those who struggle with attention issues.) So, after quickly learning how to use a paperclip to clean a microwave, I usually snap back to the task at hand.

What Does This Have to Do with Helping People Reach Their Professional Goals and Have Revenue-Generating Ideas More Often?

I'll answer with questions.

- How important are breaks? Not just lunch breaks or coffee breaks.

I'm talking about necessary rest.

- Does the relationship with a client need a rest?

Probably. But what if the month or quarter is ending and the sales professional feels pressure to reach out to that client?

As a society, especially those who are in charge of others, such as managers, I think that we should reframe how we think of not thinking about the task at hand. I used the phrase "catch its breath" earlier in reference to neural activity. After a sprinter completes a heat or a weightlifter a set, they must rest. Isn't it the same with employees who might be working for long stretches on the tasks that others have given them?

Meaning, Plain and Simple

So back to life hack videos and the academic definition of creativity. An important concept that we must discuss is the magnitude of the idea. Imagine a spectrum. On the one side, we have Big-"C" ideas such as the internet, Coltrane's jazz, and the Theory of Relativity. On the other side, we have Little-"c" ideas that are found in life hack videos.

Should a good idea be measured on the size of its impact?

Well, Should It?
That is a common theme among quite a few cognitive psychologists who study creativity. This idea builds on the concept that was discussed in **Exercise 11 ("Academic Definition")**. In that exercise, we explored the idea that a good idea is measured in the overlap zone between novelty and usefulness.

I think there is a temptation for us to be greedy, to want the big-C ideas. This is especially true for those of us who get stuck worrying about deadlines. It's as if we need the big solution *right now*.

We can liken the arrival of a big-C idea to a heroic effort or momentous occasion that somehow saved the day. We forget that the game-winning shot at the last second was only made possible by the pass that preceded it and the pass that preceded that. Imagine watching a soccer match, but only the last few seconds of that match. Of course, you'd get the result of the match, but you missed the game.

Does Size Really Matter?
With inviting ideas, it is much the same. Remember that we need to enjoy the process. Your subconscious might not know how effective the solution it brings you is any more than a faithful dog understands that some sticks it might retrieve are more crooked than others. So, take the crooked stick, the life hack idea, and the little-c idea. More and bigger ideas will follow.

Don't Forget
Remember that the Creativity Algorithm is based on the idea that regularly engaging in cognitive exercises called sophisms while in an alpha state will encourage the subconscious to assemble and deliver innovative ideas. I suggest that the likelihood of getting more ideas to follow the first one is increased by practicing "open monitoring meditation" which is a fancy label for relaxed engagement[12]. It doesn't have to be sitting still on a couch and wondering who put the alphabet in the order it is now. Relaxed engagement can be achieved by nearly any hobby, such as gardening or competitive but *low-stakes*, physical games.

Big Boss, Middle Boss, Your Boss

Employees might sometimes forget that their managers have managers. Those in charge feel just as much pressure as those they manage. Even CEOs report to the board, and business owners are beholden to their biggest customers. Bosses should celebrate and encourage the little-c ideas. Of course, sales managers would love to have their employees come up with a huge-C moment, similar to the moment when Dick Brams, a McDonald's employee, came up with the Happy Meal[13].

What if managers set up a mechanism or even a culture that celebrated and asked for more little-c moments? Finding a way to not get the power cord stuck in the office chair wheels might not sound like a big-C idea but consider the snowball effect that such a little-c idea might have on employees who have one less frustration to deal with every day.

If you are a manager and you required your team members to do this exercise or any of the exercises in this book, would reflecting on the sophisms in this exercise give your teammates an innovative idea right away? Quite possibly. But, this process isn't about the short term. No one can get in shape overnight. By regularly stretching and flexing your mind, creativity will flow.

TAKEAWAY FOR THIS WEEK

> It is easy for me to type this next sentence. Find a time to relax. As I write this, I have not made time for myself to relax in a few days, so I know the struggle is real. If you can't find time, then let's do it right now. Three deep breaths. After that, ask yourself to find an idea that is the smallest, littlest-c idea you can have. A new way to snap your fingers for example. Purposely make yourself think of an actual good idea that has a very small effect on the fewest number of people. Focus on a small-c idea. Write down everything that comes to mind however silly it might seem at the time. Do not let yourself worry about a Big-C idea. Guess what will happen if you forbid your unconscious from doing something. It just might do the exact thing that you forbid it to do.

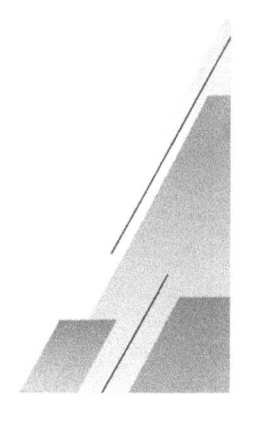

Exercise 14

TRAIN YOURSELF

What do you think of when you hear the word "train," as in "he needs more training?" Whatever you think, it probably isn't pleasant or relaxing.

I agree
I don't enjoy the phrase *"train yourself."* Don't get me wrong. Just because I don't enjoy it doesn't mean I don't value it. I firmly believe in hardcore training for certain things. In many domains, working long tireless hours is the only way to achieve what you want.

Wait. Stop!
Let me rephrase. Working long, tireless hours is the only way *to change yourself* so that you can achieve what you want. Progress doesn't come without change. When people work hard to lose weight, improve profitability, or get a promotion, what they are really working towards is changing themselves.

Wait. Wait. Stop!
Let me rephrase again. The goal isn't to change yourself; the goal is to change your brain (unless your goals happen to be related to physical

health and fitness). In later exercises, we'll dig deep into the neuroscience of creativity. There is an intricate relationship between mental events and brain functions.

Everything Changes

As you read this sentence, your brain is changing[14]. In fact, everything you do actively and everything that is done *to* you or *for* you changes your brain. Your brain is not meant to be static. The more often you do something, the more permanent the change. Of course, the brain doesn't want to be permanent; it wants to change. If you disagree with this fact, then consider why you're reading this book. Curiosity is evidence that the brain wants to change.[15]

We can guide how the brain changes. Just as gardening stakes and wires can guide how a plant grows, it is up to our mind to figure out how to help our brain grow in the right direction.

Let's Train It!

So, let's figure out a training program for your brain. Let's revisit the what-comes-first questions from **Exercise 12 ("What Comes First?")**: does regularly engaging in relaxation allow the brain to change for the better, or, rather, does changing the brain for the better allow for regular relaxation?

Relaxation

Relaxation is a skill.[16] It can be practiced. In fact, it is a *set* of skills. The more often you do it, the easier it is to do. It's as in the old adage: anything worth doing requires effort. It is strange to think that relaxing requires effort, but that is because most of us are almost constantly using our conscious mind to think, plan, anticipate, organize, and work. We have trained ourselves to do conscious, executive tasks easily and automatically.

Pause.

Think back to when you were a teenager. Were you always so conscious of deadlines, goals, time management, and to-do lists? No, you weren't.

But over time, your brain was trained to be the Type-A go-getter that is ironically driven enough to keep reading this exercise about relaxing.

Relaxation Routine

Let's establish just one relaxation routine for right now. Routines, despite how certain romantic comedy movies portray them as a warning sign of being a rigid person, are really healthy. Of course, rigidity itself isn't healthy—remember when we said the brain wants to change? So, routines should be firm, but not rigid.

> *Routine is a lazy person's way of getting things done.*
> James Clear[17]

Maybe you already have a relaxation routine. Maybe you haven't made time for it everyday. I haven't. I wish I did. I'm not going to tell you what type of relaxation exercise you should do, because I don't know what will work best for you. I will, however, say that the routine should include some key elements: uninterrupted time, slowed breathing, awareness of certain muscle groups, and something to think about. Of course, for our purposes, that something to think about is a sophism. For instance, can you envision a pan or oven that could bake crustless bread?

Take a break and think about that. That amusement and relaxation you felt was just like the feeling you had right before your last good idea. By getting into that state more often, you will invite innovative ideas to arrive more often.

I suggest including family members and friends in your plans. You shouldn't have to sneak off to eke out a few minutes for yourself. Your family doesn't (or shouldn't) bother you when you are brushing your teeth and engaging in other healthy routines. Explain what you are doing (finding a few minutes to relax and think) and why you are doing it. They will support you.

Relaxation as a Process

Practice whatever relaxation process works for you before you go to bed. Not necessarily as a way to fall asleep, but as a separate, consciousness-changing activity. I also suggest that you do it tomorrow, too. Write down when you are going to do it. Put it on your calendar. Tell people about it. The more you do it, the more likely you will do it. On a neurological level, you will be literally changing your brain.

Back to the Garden Analogy

Just as you direct a plant to grow in a certain direction, over time, that plant's stems becomes thicker and sturdier. It will eventually be able to support its own weight and continue, by itself, in the right direction.

As mentioned in previous exercises, the way to have innovative ideas frequently show up at your mind's inbox is to practice relaxed engagement. It could be working with your hobby. If you don't have a hobby, a good way to reach relaxed engagement is to regularly invite your mind to play with sophisms while being in a relaxed, alpha state.

Want a quick sophism or two?

If your thoughts could exist outside of your mind, what would they feel like if you touched them?

If someone else touched that thought that was outside of your mind, what would it feel like to your mind?

So, if you are a Type-A personality who can't relax because relaxing just gets in the way of getting everything done, then don't think of relaxing as the goal. Think of relaxing as a way to achieve your goal.

What Does This Have to Do with Helping People Reach Their Professional Goals and Have Revenue-Generating Ideas More Often?

TO ALL MANAGEMENT PROFESSIONALS

More than just *encouraging* employees to routinely relax, what if you *incentivized* it? I'm not saying take up valuable workday time with relaxation exercises, but what if you allowed for a generous prize drawing for those who submitted a relaxation log? And now let's go back to that idea of taking up valuable workday time with relaxation exercises: would it yield greater value than simply working as usual for that time? It is important that you do not connect incentivized relaxation to work endeavors. If sales professionals connect this relaxation initiative to increasing sales, they will neither relax nor increase sales.

This must be 100% process-oriented.

TAKEAWAY FOR THIS WEEK

> Use what works for you to relax. Meditation. Tea. Going for a walk. You know yourself. Then, ask yourself if thinking and behaving can physically change the brain, then what the limit of that change might be. Draw or write an answer to that question. The practical and perhaps uncomfortable takeaway is the question of how hard are you training? Reading this book is great and will yield some results. Writing in your notebook and doing the exercises will yield the results you are looking for.

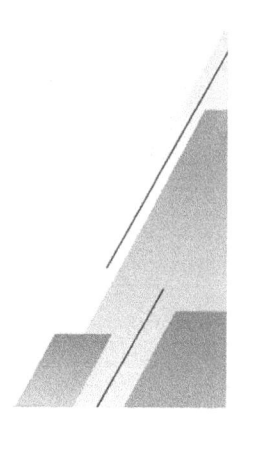

Exercise 15

BUILDING ROBOTS

Would you want a robot? Maybe one to do chores such as laundry, cooking, or dishes? I would definitely want something like that and I always have.

Looking Back

When I was a kid, I tried to build one. Growing up, we had a great workbench with what seemed like every conceivable tool there was. I was allowed, and even encouraged, to tinker.

If you have been reading this book for a while, you might wonder what was the problem? Surely, I was engaged. And I must have been pleasantly relaxed. Isn't relaxed engagement a *guarantee* for a good idea? Well, there are very few things that are guaranteed regarding the human mind.

Rules Have Exceptions

I guarantee I can get the answer to the question "What's 2+2?" to pop into your head. Did it work? No? Then, please refer to the sentence that says ***very few things are guaranteed regarding the human mind***.

Wouldn't it be great if manifesting innovative ideas were as easy as having a simply math answer be prodded into existence? That's like comparing the simplicity of a snack to the intricacy of a seven-course dinner.

And Back to Robot Building
Back to me trying to build a robot. When I was trying to build it, I'm sure the relaxation was there as I was tinkering with the spare parts I hoped to assemble into a functioning robot. Again, relaxation doesn't necessarily mean sitting on a couch. It could be the feeling an artist gets after she sits down with her easel and begins painting. Tinkering for me was—and still is—fun. Now, I mostly tinker with words and ideas.

I was engaged, but I didn't have the *right* engagement. I was trying too hard. But that wasn't the *real* reason that I didn't make any progress on my robot building. The real reason was I had no knowledge, experience, or any idea of how to reach my goal.

What Does This Have to Do with Helping People Reach Their Professional Goals and Have Revenue-Generating Ideas More Often?

Missing the Right Stuff
My young self could not build a robot despite having tools, desire, being relaxed, and having a workspace. I simply didn't have the right knowledge pieces. Do you or your team members have the right knowledge? If you're a manager, ask yourself if you can do your employee's job. I bet the answer is a resounding "yes."

If you are a sales manager, you were promoted from being a sales professional. Of course you can do the job you were promoted from. But... do you have the knowledge to do *your* job? Pause and think about that. How would you know? Were you trained in managing? If your team isn't kicking butt, might the reason be that you don't have the right knowledge?

The Right Mental Environment
One of the core ideas of the Creativity Algorithm is that relaxation coupled with the right type of mental engagement will create a mental environ-

ment that allows innovative ideas to be assembled from the subconscious. It sounds great. And it is great. It feels great to be relaxed, be engaged, and have an idea materialize with a sense of wonder and some dopamine[18].

I don't want you to assume that all a person needs to do is relax and be mentally engaged for a good idea to just magically appear. What my young mind didn't realize was that

You actually don't need just some knowledge— you need a lot of knowledge.

Expertise and Inspiration

Very few people can have a good idea that falls outside of their area of expertise. Don't believe me? Why haven't you or I made a time machine to go back and review or relive the best moments of our lives? Don't say it's because of the time paradox. If you knew enough about time travel, you might have an idea that avoids a time paradox. The simple answer is that neither you, nor I, nor anyone else has gathered enough knowledge for their subconscious to put together a good idea about time travel.

Now, Back to Legos

As mentioned in **Exercise 3 ("Gathering Legos")**, bits of knowledge are like Legos. Under the right conditions, your subconscious will play with them and put them together in new and amazing ways. Just like Legos, if there aren't enough pieces of knowledge in your subconscious, then your subconscious can't assemble a good idea.

To put it simply,

Your subconscious can't play with what it doesn't have.

Maybe I should go back and rewrite the earlier exercises. Instead of starting off with relaxation and sophisms that make people do mental double takes, like asking if sunlight is invisible, maybe I should start off with saying that in order to have a good idea in a certain domain, a person needs to know a lot about that domain.

Note:
You have never seen pure sunlight. You have only seen reflections of it from clouds, the atmosphere, the trees and anything else. Isn't it weird to think that sunlight might be invisible?

That wonder you felt when realizing you have never seen un-reflected sunlight was just like the feeling you had right before your last good idea. By getting into that state more often, you will invite innovative ideas to arrive more often.

Domain Specific / Domain Not Specific
Note also: There is debate in the scientific community about whether you need to have deep knowledge in an area before you have a good idea about that area. Some suggest that creative individuals can apply their creativity in many domains while others suggest that creativity is domain specific. Leonardo da Vinci and other "Renaissance Men" were creative in painting, sculpture, math, and engineering[19]. As you know, I like analogies. The best athletic performances often come from those who are experts who work at their craft. But the best athletes can often switch sports easily.

Into the Woods
As I write this paragraph, I wonder if the takeaway at the end of this exercise should be to encourage you to learn as much about your domain as possible so your subconscious has the knowledge to put together a good idea, OR if it should be to encourage you to practice the creative skills you've been working on. Is creativity like the scientific method, in that it can be applied to any subdomain of science, from chemistry to biology to psychology? Being scientific doesn't depend on what you study; it depends on *how* you study it. A survey, if designed and used well, can be more scientific than a fancy brain scanner.

And Out

That last paragraph got a little deep into the academic woods, so let's go back to the idea of playing. Let's give your subconscious a sophism to play with. Pretend you are about to write some code that would become the basis of a robot's mind. You want the robot to think for itself, have innovative ideas, and have free will. So, you write a bit of code that programs the robot to not follow its programming. That will give it free will right? But isn't the robot simply following instructions not to follow instructions?

TAKEAWAY FOR THIS WEEK

> As of the publication of this book, AI is in its infancy. Still, many people use it successfully to do relatively simple, repetitive tasks. What if a reader of this book thought that constantly having to come up with innovative ideas was a redundant and boring task. If you were freed from the burden of having innovative ideas and from thinking creatively, what would you replace it with? Using your notebook, make a list of some things you should know more about. Then write down one concrete way that you will gather more knowledge pieces about them.

Exercise 16:

COMFORTABLE DOING NOTHING

Did you ever have teachers that loved to pile on the homework? Similarly, did you ever have teachers that seemed to go out of their way to make students' lives difficult. I did and I intensely disliked those teachers. I bet you felt the same. As much as we might not like those teachers, let's assume that such teachers thought, however misguided they might be, that by increasing student stress they were somehow helping those students.

Let's Define Stress

Stress isn't good. It also isn't bad. It is simply a tool to change the brain. When people say they are "so stressed," their discomfort can be traced back to the idea that they didn't *choose* the type or amount of stress they feel. When I was a teacher, I stressed my students by giving them work. It was stressful because they didn't choose what the work would be, when it was due, or how to do it.

Pump Up

Happiness and growth do not come from not having stress or from having unlimited free time. If you had no stress, you would be bored—which, ironically, becomes a source of stress. Many of the happiest people you know have stress, but they *choose* their stress. Without stress, people can't grow. A micro example of this is trying to build muscle mass. Without stressing the muscle through uncomfortable workouts and allowing for proper recovery time, no growth will happen.

What Does This Have to Do with Helping People Reach Their Professional Goals and Have Revenue-Generating Ideas More Often?

Never or Not Never?
It certainly does not mean to never stress your employees, and neither does it mean to never stress yourself; rather, it means choose your stress wisely. Choose stress in a way that will change brains. As a manager who wants the best from your employees, you are responsible for changing their brains so that they can think differently. All change comes from new—and sometimes stressful—thoughts.

Brains and Healthy Growth
For many businesses, the most valuable asset isn't their employees—it's their employees' *brains*. Brains are incredibly responsive organs that literally change from moment to moment. Don't believe me? If any of the above words meant something to you, it is because your brain changed on a cellular level to process the new information.

So how do we promote healthy brain growth among employees? If you've read any or the previous exercises in this book, the answer will be relaxation and engagement. Stick with me. This is not a ploy to allow for a bigger break room or more snacks in the vending machine.

The Value of the Last 10%
This is an attempt to invite value from your employees. Notice that the last sentence didn't say "squeeze;" it said "invite." I am sure many readers will know of the diminishing results curve that occurs within employ-

ee management. Once an employee is giving 90%, getting that last 10% might not be worth what it would cost the company to squeeze it out of them,even though companies still try.

Conditional Invitations
If you have read the previous exercises in this book, then you know that, similarly, we cannot squeeze innovative ideas out of our subconscious. We must *invite* innovative ideas by creating the right conditions such as open monitoring meditation or relaxed engagement. Relaxed engagement happens when you are in an alpha state and have distracted your conscious mind with sophisms (or hobbies, or something else similarly pleasantly engaging). Let's pause and play with a sophism. This one is in the form of a true or false question.

True or false?

The human mind is the only thing to have ever named itself.

That amusement and relaxation you felt at that true or false question was just like the feeling you had right before your last good idea. By getting into that state more often, you will invite innovative ideas. We need to practice techniques that will get us there. The more often we are in that state, the more likely a transformative idea will bubble up from the subconscious.

Structured Flexibility
When I was a high school teacher, it would drive me crazy when I saw a student sitting If they didn't do the current assignment, they would be backed up when the next assignment came. It caused my hyper-organized, Type-A mind to have fits.

Duh!

At some point in my teaching career, I had an epiphany. For me, it was big; for others, it would have been greeted with a roll of the eyes and a not so quiet, "Duh!" The realization that I had had been rolling around educational philosophy for decades. It was the idea of giving students what they wanted most. It wasn't less homework; it was more time and choice.

When I implemented my epiphany, it paid huge dividends in student engagement. Suddenly, the work was *theirs*, not mine. They turned in better assignments and learned the material better. I looked year-over-year data comparing old-school micromanagement to my new approach of allowing time and choice.

Please understand it was not some New Age free-for-all. I still believed in structure. People don't produce innovative ideas in chaos; neither do they produce innovative ideas in tightly controlled, rigid environments. I gave them a choice on a few of their assignments, maybe 10-20% of them. And, as I said before, it worked.

Relax!

The metaphor I'm hoping to create is that employees are the subconscious of the business. They need to be trusted. They need to be engaged and they need time to assemble countless bits of knowledge and experience into revenue-generating ideas. How do you give time to the subconscious? By telling the conscious (management) to take a break for a while.

Relaxed engagement in management isn't new. In the early 2000s, Google had the 20% policy. This was the idea that employees were to take a break from their regular responsibilities and work on something engaging for 20% of their time on the clock.[20] Did it work? I don't know. We'll address that in a few paragraphs. What I do know is that Google AdSense, Google News and Gmail are reported to have come out of that initiative.

Google isn't the only company to do that, and they certainly were not the first. The technology company 3M did this long before Google. They had their "15% Project.[21]" It is hard to argue with 3M's success as a company. And the 15% Project is credited for allowing Arthur Fry to invent the Post-It Note[22]. So did it work?

Proceed with Caution!

I think we have to be careful here to not fall prey to the *post hoc ergo propter hoc* fallacy. Roughly translated, that fancy Latin phrase means "after this, therefore because of this," where one assumes that if one event follows another, the first event must have caused the second. Would Post-It's or Gmail have been invented without these policies? No one can say for sure. The causality of innovation is a tricky thing.

What we are sure of is that innovative ideas rarely happen when people are over-stressed…or under-stressed. When determining how much stress/management to give/allow your employees or your subconscious, perhaps you should let them decide.

Just like I had to make an adjustment to my teaching mentality, where I had to be comfortable with seeing students "do nothing," I think we need to be comfortable letting our conscious mind do nothing so that our subconscious mind can take us in directions we might not have thought of. For managers and sales managers, perhaps you should give your employees—the subconscious of your company—time to think in ways you might not be able to.

TAKEAWAY FOR THIS WEEK

> Imagine what you would do if you had a day every two weeks when you were not allowed to work on your regular tasks. What would you do with it? Do you trust your subconscious enough to let it choose? It might be hesitant. After being told to sit down and be quiet so often so your conscious mind could work uninterrupted, maybe you'd have to coax out your subconscious. Will imagining, reflecting on, and even writing a list of things you would do with an extra day bring you a money-making idea? Maybe—if you are relaxed enough while doing it. The important thing is to play the long game with your subconscious. I must stress the word "game." Let your subconscious play and you will be amazed at what it delivers.

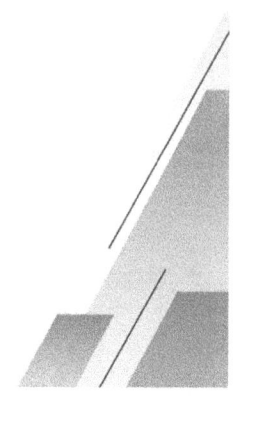

Exercise 17

THINKING WITH MUSCLES

Do you know anyone who exercises every day? I'm talking about people for whom exercise (jogging, yoga, swimming) is such a part of them that they don't even consciously think about exercise. It's just automatic,

Consciously thinking and decision making takes a lot of energy. The more routines a person has, the fewer decisions they must make and the more energy they have for other important things. People who exercise regularly don't think about —it's automatic. And they don't think *during* their exercise time. Well, at least not *consciously*.

Mindless Activity

Sometimes, I am one of those people. I have hot streaks where I get into the routine of doing daily, early morning exercises. In fact, I got the idea for this exercise while I was working out at a gym. To be precise, the ideas for this exercise bubbled up when I was returning a dumbbell to the rack. Putting a dumbbell back is a mindless task that I have done many times. I think you might see where I am going with this: it was *consciously* mindless work.

It might seem counterintuitive to think really pushing yourself physically is calming, but while you're doing it, your conscious mind is not being burdened by anything. There is simply no way to worry about deadlines while you're doing deadlifts. Work stress, returning calls, and other energy-draining thoughts cannot make it into your mind while you are physically uncomfortable. That sweet spot of having a fast-beating heart and a quiet mind is often the place where innovative ideas like to bubble up from the subconscious. Getting to that sweet spot and having ideas that increase sales can become routine.

Muscle Memory and Increased Sales

There is virtually nothing that cannot be learned so well that it becomes automatic – including prospecting, follow-ups, and closing.

Brain scans have revealed that brain activity in beginning pianists, even when playing a relatively easy piece, is much higher than in expert pianists that are playing a more difficult piece.[23] In fact, expert pianists can have an involved conversation even while they are playing a complex piece of music. They can play intricate pieces while thinking of something else because they have practiced so much it is automatic. We need to make the skills associated with selling become automatic.

How'd They Do That?

Will this work for the skill of having innovative ideas? Yes. I know of a few professional "ideaists." I would argue that for Stephen King, Malcom Gladwell, and Adam Grant good ideas are automatic. As mentioned before, there must be some level of expertise in the area where you hope to have a good idea. What these authors write happens only after exhaustive work in their areas or expertise and significant time in relaxed engagement.

The intriguing question is

What is their routine for coaxing ideas from their subconscious.

Relax, Engage, Creatively Think

If you have read the previous exercises, then you might be familiar with relaxation, engagement, and sophisms. If you are not (or even if you are, but want a refresher), here's a quick recap. When a person feels a certain type of relaxation that we call an alpha state, and when they are mentally engaged in a low-stakes but enjoyable cognitive task, innovative ideas are more likely to be assembled by the subconscious. The Creativity Algorithm advocates that getting into a relaxed mental state will encourage innovative ideas to arrive more often.

What Does This Have to Do with Helping People Reach Their Professional Goals and Have Revenue-Generating Ideas More Often?

Training Routines

What can be routinized in the sales process or in the management process? What tasks can be practiced so much that they can become automatic? As a sales manager, ask yourself about your company's training routine. Does it allow a sales professional to learn to do some tasks so automatically that they can spend their time and mental effort on more important tasks?

Practice Make Perfect

As mentioned above, when first learning a skill, especially the skill of having good ideas routinely, the whole brain is active. It is difficult. It takes effort. But with sufficient practice, that neural activity becomes condensed and organized and can allow for an essentially effortless routine.

So how many instances of practicing relaxed engagement will it take to make getting a money-making idea routine? I think there are way too many variables to make that prediction for any given person. But the theory is sound and is based on another psychological concept called neuroplasticity.

That's a Fact!
Neuroplasticity is the term for how the physical brain changes in response to environmental or cognitive circumstances. That means that, over time, a person's thoughts will change their brain. [24]

I'm going to say that again because it is so amazing:

Your thoughts can change your brain.

Walk on the Wild Side
Let's use the metaphor of walking in a dense forest. At first, it is difficult. Branches are blocking the path and piles of leaves hide rocks and roots. But the second time, you can see where you walked. It still isn't easy, but at least you might remember where a hidden root is. After a while the path gets more worn and it becomes easier to use. With more use, the path becomes easier to walk. That is how learning a skill works. The more you do, it the easier it becomes. And the easier it becomes, the more you do it.

Time to practice what we're here for. Relax, give your mind something to play with, and see what pops up. Maybe it will be a solution to a sales problem. If it's difficult for you to get in a creative mindset right now, that's OK. Nothing worthwhile was ever easy. You are literally reshaping your brain to make a path for innovative ideas to get from your subconscious to your conscious. Remember, increased sales and your other goals are only one good idea away.

Fechner's Law
Let me start our next sophism with a psychological fact based on something called Fechner's Law. If you were lifting 100 pounds, you would not notice if a butterfly landed on the weight. In fact, anything under 2 pounds wouldn't be noticeable. The percentage of weight change that is noticeable is 2%. So, if you were lifting 100 pounds and your personal trainer added one pound, you wouldn't physically be able to notice that small change.[25]

All of a sudden, and without being aware, you're lifting 101 pounds. Then, your trainer adds another pound. Now, you're lifting 102 without being aware of it. After another attempt, yet another pound is added, and you lift it successfully. Here is the sophism based on this phenomenon: where will this end? If you are unaware of the change but adapt anyway, what happened in your mind?

Small Change, Big Impact

Will playing with the sophism of noticing a change in stimuli allow a good idea to arrive from the subconscious? Over time, yes. The deeper question is whether you can notice yourself getting 1% more creative.

TAKEAWAY FOR THIS WEEK

> Make an appointment with yourself for three times this week. Then reflect on whether you feel more creative after relaxing and contemplating sophisms. Write down what comes to you in the back of this book or in your notebook. Have you compared your previous entries from earlier exercises? How would you know? Is an increase in creativity like the butterfly that landed on a barbell? Deeply reflect on this concept. Just a few moments of flexing and stretching the mind will help invite your next innovative idea. After you do that, give your subconscious time; you will be impressed by what it brings you.

Exercise 18

OUT-OF-SHAPE PERSONAL TRAINER

Have you ever seen a personal trainer who doesn't look like they exercise? Have you ever been given investing advice from someone who does not seem to enjoy financial success? Those situations can be a bit awkward and can lead to questions of credibility.

Let's apply such questions to this book. Please know that I do my best to be unflinchingly honest when it comes to self-reflection. It is that kind of self-feedback that helps support growth.

Growth isn't always easy, but it is healthy.

Black and White

Having written this book about having innovative ideas, the question readers might ask is whether I've had enough innovative ideas to make me an expert. The answer is yes, but as with anything in psychology, very few things are so black and white. Talking about one's success is a tricky thing. Let me try to answer this by walking the razor-fine edge between bragging and establishing credibility.

A Bit of Biography

In late 2009, I published a fantasy novel, *Need for Magic*. The "spells" in that book are persuasive techniques that actually work in real life. While there are many fantasy novels out there, none of them are innovative enough to have "spells" that work in real life.

After the novel, I invented and patented a first aid device. It is a re-freezable finger splint. Before this device, most people's only option for an injured finger was to hold a sandwich back of ice to their finger. When I look back at when that idea came to me, I realize that it came to me in the exact way that this book describes. I had extensive knowledge of finger injuries, I was relaxed and engaged at the time the idea arrived from my subconscious.

While I am happy with the performance of Cold Cast and my novel, they did not propel me to a level of wealth where I do not need to work anymore. Still, they are profitable. With the book and the invention, I believe I've filled an empty niche and solved a problem. So, I consider that additional evidence of innovative thinking on my part.

Let me continue with this somewhat awkward chapter by saying I have done quite well professionally. That success is spread among many endeavors. Aside from my usual day job of being a psychology instructor, I earn income from book royalties, invention sales, consulting, and public speaking.

I think much of my success comes from *not* pursuing material success. Refer to **Exercise 5 ("Don't Chase Puppies")** for a refresher on why we might not want to consciously focus on getting the next innovative idea or the next level of material success. Trying too hard to get money, make a sale, or have an innovative idea isn't enjoyable. It is stressful and that is often counter-productive, especially since good ideas come when a person is in a relaxed, alpha state.

Elementary, My Dear Reader

This book is not intended to serve as a life coach, and neither is it designed to be an investigation into life goals or an investigation into whether money should be the *means* or if money should be the *end*. Rather, it is a how-to book that explains the factors in the theory that money-making ideas are assembled by the subconscious and delivered to the conscious. Sales professionals might get that extra boost in their numbers if, counterintuitively, they take a break from single-mindedly pursuing a boost in sales.

Keep Your Eye on The Prize

To further examine the importance of focus, let's use the anatomy of the retina (at the back of our eye) as an analogy. The center of the retina is densely packed with neurons called cone cells that can sense color and fine detail. They are in the center of the back of the eye so that when we stare straight ahead, like when reading this book, we can see the fine details (e.g., letters and words). However, cones don't exist in the periphery of the retina. Which means we can't see color very well in our peripheral vision, and we certainly can't read or otherwise perceive fine-grained detail with our peripheral vision.[26] Don't believe me? Hold this book to the side but stare straight ahead. You can still see it, but you can't read the text.

You might imagine the metaphor is to keep your vision focused in front and to not get distracted by looking to the side. What I haven't told you yet is that the periphery of the retina is populated by neurons called rod cells. These cells respond well to dim light. That means that, if you want to see a dim light well, don't stare at it. Instead, focus your gaze somewhere else and notice that the dim light will appear brighter as long as you don't look directly at it.

What Does This Have to Do with Helping People Reach Their Professional Goals and Have Revenue-Generating Ideas More Often?

ALONG THE STRAIGHT AND NARROW? MAYBE NOT

What if, instead of constantly staring straight ahead at your sales goals, you looked slightly off center for just a bit? Would dim things in your periphery become a bit easier to see? Probably. Might those dim things be innovative ideas? Yes. Good ideas often hide, only appearing when you stop looking for them. Professional breakthroughs don't always happen in the office during the workday.

So, let's ask a question that is also pretty good sophism:

> *If you are to take your laser-like focus off your main goal for a bit, onto what should you put it? Pause here and reflect on that question.*

My answer to the above sophism is that we should put our attention on a hobby or another interest. That is tough for many of us because we have trained ourselves that taking our eyes off our goal is somehow a major crime against achievement. As tough as temporarily focusing on a something else might be, let me offer something that is even more difficult to focus on temporarily:

Planning and Doing a Good Deed
It might be more difficult, but I know from my own experiences that planning a good deed will reap a surprising amount of creative benefits.

The planning part is the key, because planning involves *consciously* thinking. Notice that by consciously thinking about good deeds we are focusing on something *other* than consciously thinking about our professional goals. This distraction allows our subconscious to assemble and deliver good ideas and think of a way to help someone else.

Weird Planning

It might seem weird to *plan* to get distracted. But as free spirited as the subconscious might be, engaging with it, especially at the beginning of your efforts with this process, requires a plan. Effort without a plan is like trying to imagine where wind comes from. That's a pretty fun sophism, by the way.

Where's It Blowing From?

Regarding wind's origins, you can probably recall something about low-pressure areas, and maybe you can remember a weather map from the news, but envisioning wind actually starting to blow and gathering strength, or imagining where it ends, is tough to do. Don't believe me? Take a few moments and think about how and where wind ends.

By engaging in such amused relaxation, your conscious mind took a break. Your subconscious mind poked its head up and wanted to know if it was time to play. Since it wants to play so much, let's give it another sophism.

True or false?

> *The best things in life haven't been invented yet.*

Will relaxing and thinking about wind, the best things in life, or planning your next good deed cause a breakthrough in the area you know a lot about? Maybe. Remember that just because it happens after an exercise doesn't mean that the exercise caused it.

I promise you this:

Your subconscious probably will not deliver a good idea when you are actively looking for that idea.

TAKEAWAY FOR THIS WEEK

> Find time—no, make time. Effort without a plan doesn't usually lead to achievement. Make five minutes to relax for three days. Pick your days and pick your time. Then use your favorite relaxation routine. Then imagine. No; "imagine" is too easy of a word. *Envision.* Take time to develop a detailed picture or blueprint for a way to speed up or slow down wind that *does not* involve a fan. Draw or write your ideas in your notebook.

As always, play with these sophisms; then give your subconscious time to assemble a good idea. Not only will you be surprised by what it delivers to you, you will be surprised by when it delivers it to you.

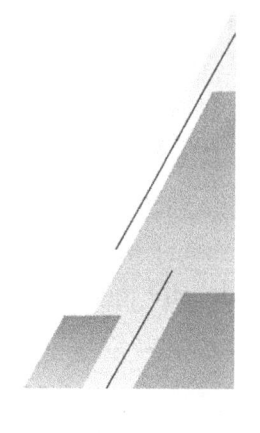

Exercise 19

IS DWI UNSAFE?

Years ago, when I was driving around, a DJ made a comment, something about "Aren't you glad no one is recording you sing as you drive?" At the time, I found it an interesting comment. It made me think of all that tasks that make up driving.

It's funny how we can do something as complex as singing in the car and still operate it safely. Or can we? Is singing while driving safe? I guess it depends on how much you are actively thinking about singing and about driving. If you are concentrating on singing, then you are not driving. You are simply aiming your car and will only start concentrating again if something grabs your attention.

Regarding the title of this exercise,

Driving while intoxicated is always unsafe.

That's a fact. No amount of sophistry or wordplay will change that.

DWIdeating

I wasn't talking about <u>d</u>riving <u>w</u>hile <u>i</u>ntoxicated. I was talking about <u>d</u>riving <u>w</u>hile <u>i</u>deating. Many of us often have good ideas when we are driving. Maybe that is because we usually drive to the same places over and over. That allows our conscious mind to take a break. The physical tasks of driving, such as turning the wheels, pressing the pedals, have become a procedural memory. See **Exercise 17 ("Thinking with Muscles")** for a deeper explanation.

So, if our conscious minds are taking a break, if we are doing something routine, and if we are relaxed, our subconscious minds might find that a good time to unexpectedly hand us a good idea. I bet it has happened to you. And maybe that isn't the weirdest place in which you had a good idea.

While this book advocates taking the slow road towards improving creativity and improving the relationship with your subconscious, if you are really in a bind and need a solution, hopping in your car and driving around might just do the trick.

THE SURPRISING PLACES OF IDEAS

Have you ever had a good idea in the shower? If so, you certainly are not alone. It makes sense. Showering, like driving, is often a comfort zone. We are usually alone, we have the temperature just right, it's something we have done for years, and it just feels good. The conditions are nearly perfect for our conscious mind to take a break. When that happens, your subconscious mind might just show you a new way it has put together information you already knew.

Two quick shower related sophisms:

- can you think of a cleaning use for waterproof soap?

- is it true that every time you clean something, you make something else dirty?

Still In the Car?
Back to the driving question—is driving while ideating unsafe? Let's phrase it like a hypothesis:

*If a person is driving and ideating,
then they are unsafe.*

The independent variable is what is done, which, in this scenario, is driving while ideating. The dependent variable is the result, which, in this case, is the level of safety.

Defined Clarification
We have a lot to pick apart. First, we need to precisely define both driving and ideating. We've defined driving well enough thus far, and we all likely have enough concrete experience with it to understand the concept. Ideating, however, is not something we have clearly described or defined yet. Ideating is a fancy term for generating ideas or solutions. It is akin to the concept of divergent thinking, which is coming up with as many solutions as possible. As mentioned in **Exercise 1 ("Introduction to the Creativity Algorithm")**, defining and measuring thoughts is nearly impossible.

Second, we need to define safe. I don't think anything can be 100% safe. So, we must look then at degrees of safety. Does taking your conscious mind off the road make driving less safe? Yes. The problem is, we can't *not* do it. Just as we know for a fact that humans cannot concentrate on more than one thing at a time, we know that humans cannot concentrate for a long time without a break. Don't believe me?

Here is another sophism.

*Start counting. How far can you go before you
get distracted and stop?*

Pay Attention!

Not being able to concentrate for long doesn't sound great when we think of highway safety. But, even when the conscious mind takes a break, it is only a split second away. In addition to being good at giving us innovative ideas, our subconscious mind is almost always scanning for danger. When it notices danger, it alerts the consciousness faster than you can think. That seamless handoff of attention is one indication of an efficient and balanced mind. Just like we can't *make* our subconscious deliver innovative ideas when we want, we can't make our conscious mind pay attention for long periods of time.

What Does This Have to Do with Helping People Reach Their Professional Goals and Have Revenue-Generating Ideas More Often?

Are your sales practices so routine that you can do them automatically? Are they as routine and effortless as taking a shower or driving a familiar route? If they are not, let me suggest that you keep working until they are. This book is not about a magical process where innovative ideas simply come out of nowhere because you are relaxed. This book is beneficial for everyone who wants/needs better roads to creative thinking. But, with years of effort, study, refinement, and practice in your area of expertise, you already have some of the necessary maps to help navigate to those great ideas.

Steps to Deliverance

If you are reading this and you are an accomplished salesperson, there are three things you can do to encourage your subconscious to deliver an innovative idea to you.

> 1. Hop in the car and go for a meandering drive where you travel familiar roads and sing songs you know well. See if a good idea will make an appearance.

2. Hop in the shower and relax. Stay in there as long as you want without guilt over wasting water or time. See if a good idea will make an appearance.

3. Find and engage in an activity that is so automatic for you that you can do it on autopilot. But make it an activity where you still have to do something.

Hide and Seek

OK, OK, enough of that. Let's get into an alpha state. One of the best ways to get into an alpha state is to get into a comfortable position, slow your breathing, and then monitor your breathing. Give yourself a few minutes to do this.

Explore and experiment how large you can expand your chest cavity when you inhale. Do it four times. Were you able to expand your chest cavity more on the fourth? Did you see what happened there? By distracting your consciousness with thinking about your chest cavity, your subconscious started to wake up, peek out, and wonder if it was play time. We need to encourage that.

The Beginning and the End

So, here is a sophism.

> *Imagine the beginning of a route you routinely drive.*
> *Really envision the beginning of your journey.*
> *Details matter. What will the air feel like?*
> *Where are the bumps in the road? Got it?*

OK, now picture the *end* of your journey. Again, work for the details. Go deep. Push your imagination. Got it?

OK, now imagine them both at the same time. Can you? Maybe not. But what was happening with the rest of your mind while you were concentrating on something you couldn't do? Again, it isn't about getting accurate images of both parts of your drive to show up simultaneously, it is about the process of flexing and stretching your conscious mind.

Did relaxing and thinking of two ends of your journey put you into an alpha state where you were mentally engaged and relaxed? If so, keep at it. If not, keep at it. That is the moment when innovative ideas are most likely to appear.

TAKEAWAY FOR THIS WEEK

> Work with expanding your rib cage as you relax several times this week. After four breaths, try to imagine the front of your car and the back of your car simultaneously. If you do that for a few seconds, you will probably get distracted because your mind needs a break from the tough task of imagining in such detail. Using your notebook, make a list of three innovative ideas you would like to have the next time you drive. Look at the list right before your next driving adventure. Give your unconscious time. See what it brings you.

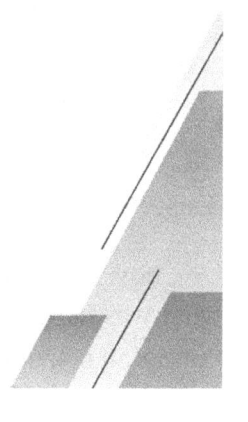

Exercise 20

DAYDREAMING IN CLASS

Wall Sitting

What's the worst physical exercise you can think of? For me, it's "wall sits." Keeping your knees bent as if you were sitting in a chair while your back is against the wall might not seem that bad – at first. Actually, I encourage you try wall sits and continue reading this exercise. See if you can use the ideas in this exercise to distract yourself from the ever-increasing discomfort in your thighs.

I learned of wall sits during the first week of wrestling practice when I was a freshman in high school. The coach blew the whistle and told the team to do wall sits. I followed along with what the older boys were doing and assumed the position. Very quickly, and I mean very quickly, my thighs started to burn. I looked around and the other guys didn't seem to be bothered by this. Eventually, the coach blew the whistle to stop the drill, and the team collapsed in exhaustion. While my legs recovered quickly, that event stuck with me.

Mental, Yes, Physical, Not So Much

Here's why: my mental will to do something ran headfirst into the physical restrictions of my body. Wanting to not embarrass myself met its match in the chemical reactions that were happening in my leg muscles. In a later exercise, we'll discuss the fascinating and limited way that our mental life can manifest in the physical world.

The Price of Attention

Physical exhaustion is not the only type of exhaustion. There is mental exhaustion. But unlike when the body is exhausted, the exhausted mind doesn't simply collapse. It can switch into a different mode of activity – which brings us to daydreaming.

Daydreaming is not only *not bad*, I think it is good and necessary. Daydreaming happens when the brain shifts from beta-wave focus to alpha-wave relaxation. In this state, the brain is still doing something. It is creating, even if that creating seems as mundane as remembering something on your to-do list.

What Does This Have to Do with Helping People Reach Their Professional Goals and Have Revenue-Generating Ideas More Often?

THEN VS NOW

Modern workplaces are not as draconian as those of the industrial era, with the assembly lines of past generations. In most modern workplaces, employees can find a way to sneak off to take a break, check their phone, and maybe daydream a bit. But, maybe, just maybe, they shouldn't have to *sneak* off. Many workplaces used to have an employee lounge. Some even had designated smoking sections.

I have not heard of any workplace having a designated daydreaming space. There are two reasons for this. The first is cultural. Organizations abhor what they perceive as idleness. The rebuttal to that type of thinking is the quote by Aaron Sorkin, "*You call it procrastinating, I call it think-*

ing.[27]"

Even if there were a designated daydreaming space, I don't think it would work very well. Going to a daydreaming area within one's place of work would be a purposeful act. For many people, daydreaming can't be done on command. (Note: daydreaming is a skill that should be practiced regularly. Regular practitioners can not only daydream on command, they can write, produce, and star in their own daydream stories.)

Industrial/Organizational psychologists can calculate the relationship between minutes spent actively working and productivity. Hint: no one is productive every minute they are at work. Within industrial/organizational psychology there is evidence that taking a few minutes off from working consistently and then re-engaging in work will lead to greater productivity.

Break Time!
Speaking of taking a break, let's take a break from discussing workplace practices. Here is a pretty easy sophism for you: if the conscious mind must take breaks, then where does it go when it takes those breaks? Does it vanish and reform? Does a part (as in thing) of your mind go to another part (as in space) of your mind when it wants to take a break? How many parts (both things and spaces) of your mind are there?

That amusement and relaxation you felt when pondering parts of your mind was just like the feeling you had right before your last good idea. By getting into that state more often, you will invite innovative ideas to arrive more often.

I don't know where your conscious mind goes when you daydream, but I know what fills the void. When your conscious mind takes a break during daydreaming," the subconscious gets to have a turn.

The Stuff of Daydreams
Now, let's make it a real sophism.

Take a minute and visualize your conscious mind taking a break. What did you see?

Notice that it was your subconscious that supplied the details of your visualization. In a later exercise, we might discuss whether you can daydream with smells, touches, and tastes. Or, maybe try it now as another sophism.

If daydreaming is when your subconscious takes over, then we should practice it. But before we run headlong into the amorphous world of the subconscious, let's ask a question.

If the subconscious takes over, what does it take over?

The Answer to That Question
To answer that, I'd like you to remember or imagine the last time you walked into a room and forgot why you entered. It's quite a common experience. Notice that for a few seconds, your body was walking unconsciously. Your subconscious is easily able to take over automatic behaviors. (**See Exercise 17, "Thinking with Muscles"**). Now, envision that. Do your best to create a mental picture of what happens in your mind when you take a few steps through a doorway and you don't know you are doing it.

Back to the Present
Notice that you do not notice when your subconscious takes over with its dreamy, feel-good alpha waves. You only notice when you come back to reality with the crisp, fast-moving beta waves. When I lecture about consciousness in my classes, I often ask students to keep track of how many

times they zone out. Of course, they can't because if they do, they are not zoning out. So, I ask them to keep a tally of how many times they *come back* to the present.

I think any sophism involving consciousness shifts is a difficult one, but, it is worth playing with. Can you create a mental model or picture of what happens in your mind when *you* turn off? That's a trick question. You don't ever turn off, because your subconscious is just as much you as your conscious self. Still, it is a good sophism

Here's where the benefits of the sophism start to stack on top of each other. By concentrating on a new mental task, such as imagining the shifting interaction between your conscious mind and your subconscious mind, you will be tiring yourself mentally. But, unlike the younger me doing the wall sits, don't give up. Keep pushing yourself. Your conscious mind will become exhausted, requiring your subconscious mind to take over. That relaxed, engaged alpha state is where innovative ideas come from, and, as we've mentioned many times, your professional goal is only one good idea away.

TAKEAWAY FOR THIS WEEK

> Of course, you should plan out three sessions where you will allow yourself to relax. The sophisms in this exercise are not something to be played with and forgotten in anticipation of next week's exercise. Using your notebook, create, draw, or describe a model of what happens in your mind when you shift consciousness. Writing or sketching is an exercise that will have many benefits as we continue this journey. If you can create a detailed model of how your mind works, then you will be in a great position to invite innovative ideas very often.

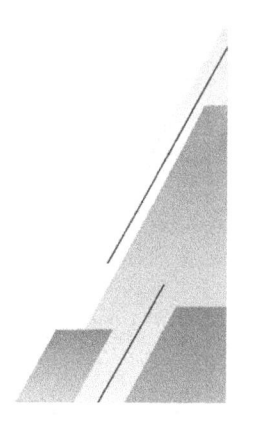

Exercise 21

BOWLING BALLS AND BLANKETS

Have you ever watched "A Christmas Story?" If you know it, you'll know that the main character, Ralphie, often daydreams, and at least one of his dreams involves protecting his family from bandits with his much hoped-for Red Ryder BB gun. Let's pause our exploration of daydreaming for now and go to something heavier. Don't worry, we'll come back to Ralphie.

$E=MC^2$

Allow me to discuss my very limited understanding of Einstein's Theory of Relativity. As I understand it, objects that have a huge amount of mass, like stars, can bend spacetime.[28]

As I said, I barely understand it, but I can pass along the blanket analogy that's sometimes used to explain it.

$E=MC^2$ In Layman's Terms

Imagine that a blanket is held taught by its corners by four people. Imagine that it is about 3 feet off the ground and pulled so tight that there are no wrinkles. Now imagine that a bowling ball is placed on the flat, wrinkleless surface. The ball will sink down into the blanket and the blanket will stretch as the weight of the ball settles in. This represents an object with a lot of mass bending spacetime.

Now imagine that another ball is dropped at a different location on the blanket. That new ball is a ping pong ball. It has very little mass, at least compared to the bowling ball. While it might sit still on top of the blanket for a while, eventually, and with the help of a little jiggling from the blanket holders, that ping pong ball will fall into the impression that is caused by the mass of the bowling ball. This is not unlike how the massive Earth pulls a relatively un-massive apple towards it.

THE DEFAULT NETWORK

OK, before I explain why I took time to write about the blanket model of how gravity is bent spacetime, let me talk about a term in psychology called the "**default network**." Basically, it means that we usually think about the same types of things when our mind is idle.[29] A common default network is to think of all the things on your to do list. Many organized, motivated adults are in a perpetual cycle of thinking of things to do, putting them on a list, and getting them done. That is their default network.

Another common type of default network involves anxious thoughts. An anxious person's idle mind is drawn to worry. And the more often they think of worrisome thoughts, the easier it becomes to think such thoughts.

And the Blanket?

OK, now back to the blanket. Imagine that your default network is the large bowling ball and that your subconscious is the light, hollow ping pong ball. If your default network usually thinks of more things to get done, then when your mind is wandering, your subconscious thoughts will be drawn to the weighty default network of thinking of more things to do. Sadly, the same is true with those who struggle with anxiety, depression, and other things with huge psychic masses: the subconscious will often fall into the impression that the heavy default network makes.

What Does This Have to Do with Helping People Reach Their Professional Goals and Have Revenue-Generating Ideas More Often?

If you had to guess, what is the default network of the employees in your organization? Relaxed and confident in their ability to do well? Constantly nervous about falling into an impression caused by something with more mass such as the demands of an unreasonable boss?

Reaching the Next Level

Remember it is very difficult to have a good idea when the mind is stressed and rushed. And as we know, innovative ideas can help companies reach the next level. It is foolish and wasteful to sit around and wait for only those in management to have innovative ideas. Smart organizations know that employees are more than mere automatons that carry out tasks; they are idea-fountains. If you are an employee, how can you pass along your innovative idea to management?

I started this exercise talking about how Ralphie in "The Christmas Story" constantly daydreams. For him, daydreams are automatic and common. Let me suggest that on the blanket of his mind, the ball with the most mass, the ball that is pulling in all the other balls is his positive imagination. That's why it is so easy for him. It can be that easy for us too.

The Challenge of Creative Imagination

Before we talk about how to make creative imagining easy for us too, let me suggest we all might have a few bowling balls on our blankets, likely of varying sizes and weights. You probably know that not all of our bowling balls are particularly pleasant. And that's OK. This isn't a mental health book, but it is important to take a sentence or two to say that having a certain number of recurring, unpleasant thoughts is normal. If, however, those thoughts cause distress or impaired functioning, I would strongly advise you to get help.

Having said that, it doesn't mean the negative bowling balls have to be the biggest or heaviest. We can change the mass of the bowling balls of our minds. That way, the roaming ping pong ball of our subconscious will be more likely to fall into the impression caused by the ever-growing bowling ball of innovative ideas. And that's what we want to make it: ever-growing. We want the process of having innovative ideas to be our default network. So, how do we do it? Sophisms.

Let's play with a few sophisms help make that the creativity ball have more mass.

- If everything is made of atoms, what are shadows made from?

- Flames don't cast shadows. Shine a flashlight on a campfire and you will not see a shadow. Is that because the flame of a campfire is not dense enough? Could there ever be light that is so dense, it can make a shadow if illuminated by another source of light?

(In case you started this book with this exercise, a sophism is a creativity exercise. It is a playful challenge designed to flex and stretch the mind. It is best played with when a person is in a relaxed state of mind.)

GROWING YOUR THOUGHTS' GRAVITATIONAL PULL

Weird Stuff Creation

Plan your daydreams. Think of a quick story. Maybe even a storyboard or a one-page comic book. The weirder the better. Make that the sophism for this week and weeks beyond. It might sound a bit weird to plan a weird daydream. Do it anyway.

For your daydream, push yourself out of your comfort zone. Let your child-like mind run wild without fear of judgement. Your imagination is the most private part of you; don't place limits on it. If you do, it might affect the arrival of future innovative ideas. No one is looking, so have fun. Be uncommon.

Will this exercise guarantee that you will have a good idea? I don't think anything about the subconscious can be guaranteed. Working with this process over time, however, will invite your subconscious to work/play with you more often. Since good ideas come from the subconscious when it is playing, the more you play with it, the more likely it will give you a money-making idea.

Don't believe me?

Can you tell me or even yourself what your next four thoughts will be? I bet you can't.

That is cool sophism—trying to predict your future thoughts. Did you notice how difficult that is? That is your *conscious* mind. You have a little bit of control over your conscious mind; you have *no* control over your subconscious mind. You can't predict even *one* future action of your subconscious mind.

Play Time

So, we can't guarantee anything, but we can encourage the subconscious mind to play. To do that, we need to give it things to play with and time to play. The toys that your subconscious plays with are your experiences, memories, perceptions, and emotions. But maybe, just maybe, your subconscious is like a puppy that is bored with all of its old toys. Let's give it some new, uncommon toys by purposely daydreaming.

TAKEAWAY FOR THIS WEEK

> In your notebook, write a short mental script of what you will daydream about. Then sit down and engage in a few short breathing exercises. After you have relaxed your body, spend 10 minutes working on your daydream. Add details, extra scenes, and even a few guest stars. Tell your logical, judging conscious mind to take a break for a bit. I bet you'll really enjoy it. Just a few moments of flexing and stretching the mind will help invite your next innovative idea. After you do that, give your subconscious time; you will be impressed by what it brings you.

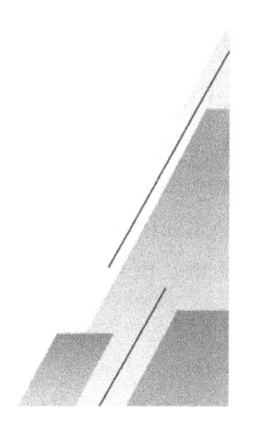

Exercise 22

IMPATIENT CEOS

Let me start by saying the title of this exercise is not a dig at business leaders or decision-makers whose responsibility it is to make more money. I respect anyone who runs a business of any size. It is a much harder job than many employees think it is.

Bosses, Bosses, Ad Infinitum

Everyone has a boss, even the boss. Those at the top of the ladder still report to boards of directors, shareholders, customers, and the public. That's a lot of people to please, so everyone, including your boss, makes the best decision they can with the information they have. The Creativity Algorithm's purpose is to help increase value by encouraging leaders and employees to have innovative ideas more often.

When I give keynote speeches at different events or when I do smaller workshops for organizations, a company is investing in me. I take that seriously, not only for the surface-level idea that I want to protect my professional reputation, but also for the deeper ethical level.

Time and energy are finite, precious resources. If people and companies are going to invest time and effort into the idea that regularly going into an alpha state will help have innovative ideas more often, I want the exercises I've written help them frequently do that.

Few things are more frustrating than the feeling of having one's resources wasted. Quite simply, I care about people, even more so when they place their trust in me.

One Idea Equals How Many Dollars?
When I negotiate with event planners or business leaders about giving a speech or leading a training session, they want to know what they will get. They want numbers. They think some version of the question, "How many innovative ideas per dollar spent can we expect?"

Fair Question
I'm careful with my money. When I spend money on something, I want to know what I will get. Incidentally, this is why so many folks are hesitant to give money to desperate people on the street asking for a dollar. It's not because those with money are mean or uncaring. There's more to it than that. Aside from the obvious ingroup/outgroup bias, with the panhandler not being part of "their" group, people are afraid to give a dollar because they don't want their resources wasted.

Place an Ad, Make Money?
Let's talk about advertising. Before they spend money on advertising, decision makers must ask or try to quantify how many new customers and new sources of revenue they will get if they spend their organization's resources on advertising. Those are good questions. But, I have yet to see an advertising sales professional *guarantee* a certain number of new customers or guarantee a certain increase in revenue.

Advertising is an attempt
to change minds.

THE CHALLENGE OF CHANGING MINDS

And that brings us to the Creativity Algorithm. We are here to change minds on many levels. Changing the conscious mind is difficult enough; trying to do it with the subconscious mind is, well… maybe it is *not* difficult if we think of our subconscious as a partner and not an employee.

Psss…Did You Hear?

Ask a marketing or advertising expert about that. There are plenty of semi-substantiated rumors that it takes an average person seeing a message seven times before something in their mind changes. Just typing that made me wince a bit as a research psychologist who appreciates the precision of specific research findings. I Googled it and found quite a few sites that support this Rule of Seven, so it must be true. Wink.

Dependent/Independent Variables

So how many sophisms must a person ponder before they get their next revenue-generating idea? And would the good idea have happened without pondering sophisms? Finding a cause in psychology is nearly impossible. I've said it before, if psychology were easy, we'd call it any other science. For example, chemistry has a neat, organized table where everything is in its place. A helium molecule is the same as every other helium molecule, so we know how it will interact in every situation. In psychology, there are simply too many variables between people and within people for us to predict that any one independent variable will cause a change in the dependent variable.

Even though psychological outcomes can't be predicted as accurately or as specifically as outcomes in chemistry, we do still have strong general ideas about how people will react and behave. Yes, working with the Creativity Algorithm is an investment of time, but it's a wise one, for it is founded on robust, well-supported psychological principles. It's a wise investment not only for the business leader personally, but for his company. One would hope they would also engage in the activities for themselves and not just hire a speaker or consultant to train their employees. Maybe

I should put an addendum on my next consultant contract saying that the CEO or owner must agree to provide evidence that he routinely engages in the exercises and encourages their employees to do the same.

Small Benefit, Big Value

The snowball effect is a term for how a small increase in a benefit will become an increasingly big benefit. I prefer, but am hesitant to use, the idea of compounding interest. The snowball effect is vague and leaves wiggle room in terms of specificity. Compounding interest raises the question of what the rate of increase is.

What Does This Have to Do with Helping People Reach Their Professional Goals and Have Revenue-Generating Ideas More Often?

Convergent Solutions

Convergent solutions are ones that use a common sense, straightforward answer rather than an out-of-the-box elaborate idea.[30] Let's consider a very mundane convergent solution to a problem that affects a single employee: a cord that stretches from her desk to the receptacle on the wall next to her keeps getting caught in the wheels of her desk chair. She can't control where the receptacle is or what type of office chair she was assigned. But she might be able to move her desk, tape the cord, or get a chair mat so that the cord does not have to run along where her chair wheels are. That small, good idea has allowed her to remove a source of stress, and stress, as discussed in a prior exercise, is an effective blocker of innovative ideas.

What might her mind think of next now that she feels a bit more relaxed and feels like she has a bit more control over her situation? Might she then think of a way to re-think how she processes emails so that she can catch out-of-date information being forwarded to another department? By not having to deal with the calls from the department that received the out-of-date information, what might her more relaxed subconscious put together when her conscious mind needs a break and wanders off?

Imagine this scenario playing out throughout a whole organization. It is that kind of ever-increasing improvement that compounding innovative ideas can cause.

What I've described sounds great—so great in fact that CEOs and sales managers often want the benefits right away. As I said before, everyone has a boss they're looking to please. However, the subconscious may or may not have a sense of time, and if it did, it probably wouldn't align with corporate schedules.

That doesn't mean it can't be speeded up.

Faster, Faster!

To the sales managers who are reading this, ask your personal financial planner to speed up the results of your personal investments. See what they say. Your financial planner can't hurry the growth of your investments outside of a certain relationship to the indices. If they can, please contact me! With training, however, your subconscious *can* hurry the growth and delivery of money-making ideas. It's just that it doesn't know or care about your schedule. It simply wants to play.

Nibble on this Sophism

So, let's give it a sophism to play with. When eating a sandwich, it's pretty universal that the thumbs hold the bottom of the sandwich. But let me ask you this:

*When you pick it up from the plate, do you slide your fingers under the bottom of the sandwich and flip it,
or do you slide your thumbs underneath
and keep it upright the whole time?*

Ultimately, nearly everyone ends with their thumbs in the same position, but how many of us start in that position?

That amusement and relaxation you felt when thinking about picking up a sandwich was just like the feeling you had right before your last good idea. By getting into that state more often, you will invite innovative ideas to arrive more often. Remember...

> *Increased sales—or whatever your goals might be—*
> *are only one good idea away.*

TAKEAWAY FOR THIS WEEK

> First things first: relax. For many, that is difficult. Plan to sit down, be mindful of how tense your muscles are, and do some breathing exercises. Ideally, this is something you will do this often. After you feel an alpha state start to develop, reflect on whether unexpected surprises and good luck are better than expected and planned for rewards. Jot down your thoughts, even if they have nothing to do with this week's sophism. Just a few moments of flexing and stretching the mind will help invite your next innovative idea. After you do that, don't be an impatient CEO. Give your subconscious time; you will be impressed by what it brings you.

Exercise 23

CHRISTMAS VACATION

What do you think about vacations? Or Christmas? Chances are you have not only some great memories but also the tingle of anticipation as your imagination starts to assemble what might happen in the future. And, because this is the Creativity Algorithm, we are going to tap into that imagination.

Take a Break

There is a way to harness the power of vacations and holidays even when you are at home or in the office and overwhelmed with too many mundane tasks. Not every day can be Christmas or a day at the beach, but there doesn't have to be such a binary divide. By that, I mean 0 equals no vacation ever and 1 equals always on vacation all the time. Neither is ideal, but the good news is that it doesn't have to be one or the other. That is, it doesn't have to be 1 or 0. Maybe you could be ½, or any of the other infinite number or numbers between 0 and 1 (see Exercise 6, "How Many Numbers Are There?").

If you love Christmas, or if you look forward to a vacation, you know that the time *before* the event is magical. I am a Christmas nut. I am writing this in February, on a plane heading for a vacation. As I left this morning, my garage was still decorated with Christmas trappings. As a researcher, I do find it hard to precisely identify what it is about Christmas time or the excitement of packing for vacation that makes both so enjoyable.

Warm, Fuzzy, Dopaminergic Reality

Let's counterbalance the warm-fuzzies of this Christmas discussion with a bit of hard-nosed science, specifically neuroscience. You might have heard that, of the over 100 brain chemicals that have been identified, dopamine is the one most related to anticipation and reward.[31] Neurochemically, we use the term dopaminergic to describe the dopamine-driven excitement of this time of anticipation. Was that sentence boring? OK, let's say that we would also use that word to describe the time *before* sex.

Wanting Is Better Than Having?

I think many people might agree that the time *before* Christmas is better than the time after and you would probably agree that it is true of sex as well. That might seem counterintuitive. After Christmas is when you have the presents you wished for, but that points to role of dopamine and the pleasure we get from *anticipation*. Once we have the presents (or whatever else we've been waiting for), that anticipation drops, and the dopamine along with it. There is also a noticeable drop in dopamine levels after orgasm. So, in a weird twist of the mind, wanting is better than having, and before is better than after.

So, Before Is Better?

This is true of the subconscious and innovative ideas. If you are reading this book regularly and doing these exercises, let me challenge you to focus on the *before*. The "before" is the time of possibility, of anticipation; it is the process. The "after" is the result.

If we focus on the *process* of getting innovative ideas, we will stay in the zone of playing with our subconscious in a relaxed state. If we switch to thinking of the "after," a mindset that is focused on having, then we lose the very thing that will bring us the good idea.

Am I asking you to plan and look forward to a vacation, only to change your plans and postpone the vacation so you have more anticipation time?

No, of course not. But would that be so bad? If a vacation is postponed, you would still have your future vacation *and* have even more "before time" to enjoy dreaming about it.

What Does This Have to Do with Helping People Reach Their Professional Goals and Have Revenue-Generating Ideas More Often?

MORE IS BETTER

Increased sales are the result. In fact, they might be the only result that matters. Remember, results are the product of the process. I am not saying that we shouldn't have sales professionals focus on results, but it shouldn't be binary, like 1 and 0. They can focus on the result *and* the process. The process brings the product. By focusing on the "before" of a sale, the sales professional might be more likely to close that sale. The "before" can be anything from getting to know your client better to ensuring your fulfillment department is ready for a large impending sale.

Don't believe me that things are better before the vacation or before Christmas? Quickly think of five Christmas songs. It shouldn't be too hard. Are any of them about the time *after* Christmas?

The Beauty of the "Before"

What makes a vacation getaway great? As we discussed, a big part of it is the anticipation. The beginning is very cool, too. It is full of possibilities. Relaxation. Escapism. Adventure. However, I don't think anyone likes the end of the vacation, the journey home, the unpacking clothes. Similarly, I don't think many people like packing up the decorations after the holiday.

What if, just what if, the thing that makes a vacation great is what you *think* about it? Vacations happen in the mind, not on the beach, in the mountains, or at the resorts. Many people love Christmas even though they don't get presents or have decorations.

Location, Location, Location?
There are plenty of people who live and work at the beach, in the mountains, at resorts, and in other vacation spots, and they are not on vacation. So, location does not dictate vacation. If it isn't the presents and decorations that dictate Christmas, and if it isn't the location or the lack of work that dictates vacation, then what is it?

Better Before or After?
The magic of Christmas is in the mind, *before* the presents. The excitement of sex comes before the orgasm, in the mental excitement of the build up to the moment. The magic of vacation is in the mind, not in the location. Very few people consciously and meticulously assemble their Christmas, sexual, or vacation fantasies. They just kind of appear in the conscious mind. And I bet you can guess from where.

Remember Your Phone Number?
Let's try something. I'd like you to try to remember your phone number. OK, now a family member's number. Easy right? Embedded in that activity is the inverse of the question from the phone number sophism in **Exercise 7**. In that sophism, we asked where the phone number "goes" when we think about something else; this time, the question is about where the phone number originates. Where are these numbers when we're not thinking of them, and where do we "pull" them from? That's an interesting little sophism.

That amusement and relaxation you felt was just like the feeling you had right before your last good idea. By getting into that state more often, you will invite innovative ideas to arrive more often. Remember, increased sales—or whatever your goals might be—are only one good idea away.

And Now Christmas?
Now try to remember the time right before Christmas or before a vacation. Not as easy as remembering the phone number, is it? Why? The short answer is that phone numbers and pre-vacation thoughts are very different mental events with very different qualities. How they are stored in the brain and where they are stored in the brain are very different from each other.

Remembering the "before" isn't easy. But it is possible. When you just tried to remember your last vacation, maybe all that you got was just a glimpse. A flash. Then, it was gone. But, like I said in **Exercise 1 ("Introduction to The Creativity Algorithm")**, the brain is flexible.

Back to the Woods
The analogy of a path in the woods to describe brain flexibility was introduced **in Exercise 17 ("Thinking with Muscles")**. Let's revisit it here. Imagine that learning a new skill is like walking on a barely-traversed path in the woods. It's difficult and slow, but the more you walk along it, the easier it gets. If you can eventually learn to remember the goodness that existed before a vacation or holiday, why can't that happen with the goodness that comes before a good idea? Remember,

Practice might not make perfect, but it does make progress.

The Before
For management professionals, don't just allow time off because you are required to allow it. What if you asked one of your team about their vacation? Not the obligatory, "How was your trip?" with its undertones of, "Now get started on everything that has piled up since you've been gone." What if you asked them before they go? Show them that you are interested in where they are going. Help them engage in the *"before."* Notice how their mental set will change.

In this exercise we have introduced the concept of the *"before."* Let go back in time to almost the first before for a few fun sophisms.

- When does a baby have its first thought?

- Prenatal EEG scans show that an unborn baby has brain activity that is just like dreaming. What could an unborn baby who has never seen, tasted, touched, or smelled anything dream about?

TAKEAWAY FOR THIS WEEK

> Be purposeful in your attempt to find an alpha state. As much as I've talked about the "before" of Christmas and the "before" of vacation, those times are often very busy and require a lot of work. For this week, please take three mini vacations. Find a spot to sit or lie down. Work on your breathing. Work on relaxing your shoulders and facial muscles. Then find the "before" of whatever vacation or holiday you are looking forward to. Write a short description of what anticipation feels like. Of course, by getting in an alpha state, and focusing on the before of an future or imagined event, you are actually practicing the before of a good idea.

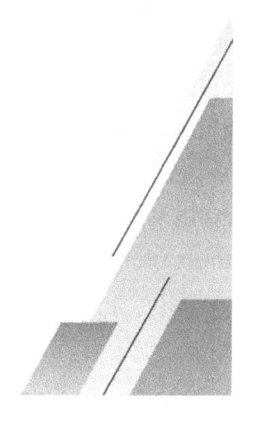

Exercise 24

MUSCULAR BAG OF ACID

Do you have something or a trigger that makes you nervous? If so, that is normal, natural, and… a bit nonsensical. I mean if we all have things that make us nervous, then we know about them. They are known quantities. We should have gotten used to them by now. Right?

If you agree, that is your *conscious* mind talking. Your conscious mind for all of its organization ability, doesn't have a lot of control over emotions or imagination.

For example, I consciously know from years of experience that getting blood drawn for my annual physical or for donating blood doesn't actually hurt—at least not enough to be afraid of it. Still, I feel the nerves rise up. Why can't I prevent the increase in heart rate or sweating. I hate the fact that I can't.

Hate Those Butterflies!

You know what else I hate? The other symptoms of nervousness. The ones I get right before I am about to give a speech. Which makes no sense at all, because I chose to become a public speaker. I bet you can guess the other symptoms. One common one is what people call butterflies in your stomach.

Butterflies in our stomachs brings me to the title of this exercise. Really, our stomach is a muscular bag of acid that can be as small as our fist or as big as several fists. So, why, oh why, does our stomach, which is a muscular bag that contains acid strong enough to eat through that same bag that holds it, feel nervousness?

Hmm?

Let's think about that. Does the stomach *feel* the nervousness? How can it? It doesn't have the neural structures that allow it to process fear. Those exist in the brain. So...

> *How can you feel fear in a body part that doesn't have the ability to feel that emotion?*

That's a pretty cool sophism.

Everything Amygdala[32]

Yes, we *do* feel fear in our stomachs. When we think about consciously it, it makes no sense. It is the subconscious we're talking about after all; it's not going to make sense to our conscious mind. The ability to feel fear existed well before humans were on the scene evolutionarily. At least we think it did. We can't prove that the elephant's distant cousin, the mammoth, felt fear, nor can we prove dinosaurs felt fear, but based on modern reptiles, we assume so. Even reptiles have a brain structure called the amygdala, which is thought of as the fear center of the brain.

> *It's intriguing to think that fear existed before humans were there to experience it.*

So, as a sophism:

> *Did your feelings exist before you did?*

If we believe that humans are the only animals to have evolved consciousness, then we must assume that fear came before the ability to understand it.

Here is a sophism. We can probably agree that the number of thoughts you can have are nearly infinite. Multiply that by the billions of people who live now and have ever lived

It is it safe to say that you've had some thoughts that no one else has ever had. Is the same true of emotions?

Nope? Maybe? Maybe Not

I don't think so. I think there are a very limited number of emotions. By that logic, it is possible that a mammoth or dinosaur felt your feelings before you did.

Will reflecting on whether dinosaurs feel the same type of fear as you give you an innovative idea right away? Maybe, but this process isn't about the short term. No one can get in shape overnight, but...

By regularly stretching and flexing your mind, creativity will flow.

THE RIDER AND THE ELEPHANT

Nervousness happens when our subconscious thinks something is important. A recurring theme of the Creativity Algorithm is that we should *listen to* and *work with* our subconscious. That is where emotional health and innovative ideas come from: working with our subconscious. The opposite is true when we ignore our subconscious or try to control it.

I am certainly not saying that we should try to dive into a fake version of our subconscious to try to find out what the "real" reason is for our anxiety. Even if you or I were trained in that specific type of psychotherapy, we probably shouldn't do it on ourselves. We don't do our own dentistry, so why should we try to do our own therapy?

So, let's work *with* our subconscious when it steers us into nervousness, anxiety, and fear. The reality is that we don't have much of a choice. Let's use Jonathan Haidt's metaphor of the rider and the elephant.[33] Imagine you are riding a 13,000-pound elephant. Maybe it was your life's dream. Maybe you traveled to a place where they have such opportunities for tourists to ride elephants (which ethically is pretty shaky) just so you could do it. Or, maybe you work with elephants or even a specific elephant every day. You're sitting up there, in the saddle, you have the reins, and you are ready to go. Except the elephant decides to go in a different direction. What are you going to do about it?

The Rider/Elephant Analogy

The rider is the conscious mind and the elephant is the subconscious. Who's really in charge? Ah, but that is the wrong way to think of it. There is no "in charge." There is no boss. There is only communication and understanding. That is how to work with your subconscious when it delivers anxiety to you, and that is how to work with your subconscious when you ask it to deliver innovative ideas to you.

What Does This Have to Do with Helping People Reach Their Professional Goals and Have Revenue-Generating Ideas More Often?

Leaders and Managers, Listen Up!

For the readers who are leaders and managers of people, consider that you are the rider and that your people are the elephant. How are you going to get the best out of them? Pulling the reins tight? Letting them go wherever they want? No—to both. But, there must be a boss in most business endeavors. Similarly, who's in charge of a sales transaction? The client cannot be in charge because he doesn't have the product, and the sales professional can't be in charge because he doesn't control the money.

No Treating, Just Thinking

This exercise is not supposed to be taken as a treatment for anxiety or nerves. Rather, maybe it can help me, you, or anyone else that might read this book find a better way to *think* of anxiety. Notice I said "think," not "treat," "battle," or "eliminate." Anxiety isn't our enemy. It is a part of us that we shouldn't try to control. We should work with it.

Anxiety and Phobias

Anxiety—and, to some extent, phobias—might seem random and irrational, and to the conscious mind, they might be utterly nonsensical. After all, why do I still get a bit of butterflies right before a blood draw? It doesn't make sense, and I get mad at myself for it. But then I reframe my thoughts and think that anxiety happens around things that our subconscious thinks are important. Why does my subconscious think that getting my yearly blood draw is important? I don't know. I might never know. But I am going to adopt a mindset of accepting the quirks of my subconscious. The Creativity Algorithm is based on having a good, playful relationship with your subconscious.

To help cultivate this playful relationship with your subconscious, I have three sophisms for this week.

> **Sophism one:** *If your stomach feels fear and your cheeks feel embarrassment, which part of your body feels innovative ideas? Hair follicles on your arm?*
>
> **Sophism two:** Let's dip into Mayer's idea of the law of conservation of energy. Basically, energy cannot be created or destroyed. Motion can cause heat (e.g., friction creates warmth). *Heat can cause motion (e.g., steam engines). Electricity can make light (e.g., bulbs), and light can make electricity (e.g., solar panels). So...what about the energy*

of anxiety? Is it caused by chemical reactions in the brain? More importantly, and here is the sophism, can we transform anxiety into a different type of energy?

Sophism three: Einstein says that matter can be converted into energy and that energy can be converted into matter. *If thoughts are energy, can thoughts ever be converted to matter? Theoretically yes, though we do not have the process for it. The sophism is not to create the process but to imagine what the resulting matter would look like. Color? Size? Shape? What would a physical thought be made out of?*

That amusement and wonderment you felt was just like the feeling you had right before your last good idea. By getting into that state more often, you will invite innovative ideas to arrive more often. Remember, increased sales—or whatever your goals might be—are only one good idea away.

TAKEAWAY FOR THIS WEEK

> Get yourself in a nice, cozy alpha state. The sophisms are listed above. I am not suggesting that you work with all three several times this week. That's too much. In fact, pick one to *not* think of. Can you guess what's going to happen? The main thing is to enjoy. Write down your thoughts as you contemplate the sophisms. Enjoy all of your thoughts even if they arise unexpectedly from your subconscious.

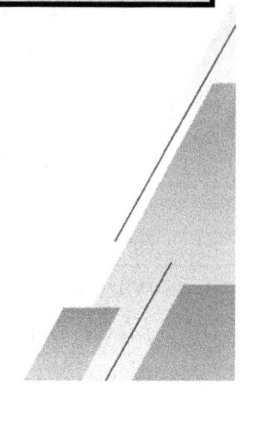

Exercise 25

FILLING OUT FORMS

Like a lot of people, I hate filling out forms, especially the repetitive ones that seem to infest the healthcare world. But—and this is where it gets weird—I like making forms. I have made plenty of educational worksheets in my time as a psychology instructor. I think there are a few reasons why I enjoy making forms.

Reason No. 1: Creative Enjoyment
First, there's the simple truth that I like making things. I like it when my ideas become tangible. That's what *The Creativity Algorithm* is after all.

To borrow a sophism from classical philosophy, I could suggest that

> *Making something, even if it is a boring, paper form, offers existential reassurance.*

If I created something, then I must exist. The creation is proof of the creator. Nothing comes from nothing.

Reason No. 2: Organization

I mentioned there were a few reasons. The second reason is based on organization. By making a form that might have a T-chart or a Venn diagram, I am attempting to organize student thoughts in an agreed-upon, standard format. Organizing, coaxing, and shaping thoughts, whether it is for themselves or others, might be one of most rewarding endeavors a person can engage in.

Let's examine the title of this exercise: "Filling out Forms." It's not really about old-school, carbon-copy forms, purple ditto worksheets, or fillable PDFs. The title is a segue to ancient philosophical ideas.

Plato's Philosophy

The Greek philosopher Plato believed that there were two worlds: the *material world* and the *form world*[34]. The *material world* is where our bodies exist. It is full of things we can touch, see, hear, taste, and smell. It can be measured and observed. However, everything in the *material world* is an imperfect representation of what exists in the *form world*, which is the realm of ideas, mathematics, knowledge, beauty, and justice.

The *form world* for Plato was the only one that mattered. Consider that you have never seen beauty itself. You have only seen limited *examples* of beauty in the *material world*, such as a painting or a landscape. Likewise, you have never seen justice. You have only seen examples, such as in a court's decision.

While the material world is made of matter and things we can touch, the form world can only be experienced through reason.

And So to Clarify

Here is an example of what might exist in the form world but cannot exist in the material world: A perfect circle. Immediately people might think they have seen a perfect circle. But, due to imperfections in paper, ink, the mechanics of a printer, and minor shimmies of earth's crust, a perfect circle cannot exist in the material world. The same can be said of beauty. We can only see examples of beauty in the material world. We cannot empirically sense the true form of beauty itself.

What Does This Have to Do with Helping People Reach Their Professional Goals and Have Revenue-Generating Ideas More Often?

CUSTOMER LOYALTY

Let's consider the true form of customer loyalty. We can't see it; we can only see examples of it. Similarly, we cannot see innovation; we can only see examples of it. Innovation and creativity exist in the form world, whereas the idea for the new sales procedure or the idea for new product exists in the material world. The bridge between them is innovative ideas. Once it comes into the material world, the new sales procedure will be implemented imperfectly.

Make It So, Epistemologists

So how do we get the form world, which is only knowable by thinking about it, into the material world where seeing is believing? That is literally the point, the goal, the mission, and the objective of the Creativity Algorithm.

Let's apply a little bit of Greek philosophy known as epistemology. We know a perfect circle exists, even though we cannot draw it or see it. Why? Well, first there is the geometric proof that many of us learned in high school and have since forgotten. Second, there is the weirder idea that a perfect circle must exist, or we wouldn't be able to think it.

By that circular logic (see what I did there?)...

> *The form of a good idea must exist because your last good idea proved it.*

If that circular logic made you do a mental stutter step and got you thinking and feeling, then I bet that feeling is just like the feeling you had right before your last good idea. By getting into that state more often, you will invite innovative ideas to arrive more often. Remember, increased sales—or whatever your goals might be—are only one good idea away.

A good idea is the juncture between the creativity of the form world and the application of the idea in the material world. We can't touch a good idea, so in that respect, a good idea must have at least one foot in the form world. But, a good idea leads to something we can touch and implement. In that way, it has one foot in the material world.

Take a Break and Reflect

The sophisms for this week have nothing to do with innovative ideas. In fact, take a break from trying to have a good idea. Of course, if you have read more than a few of these exercises, then you might know that a major theme of *The Creativity Algorithm* is to *not* chase a good idea.

The sophismd for this week reflect on questions about the form world. I'll start with a few questions, but please let your mind explore wherever the ideas take you.

- Does the form world really exist?

- How would we know if it does or doesn't?

- Is everything we see an imperfect version of its "parent" in the form world?

TAKEAWAY FOR THIS WEEK

> I'm going to be transparent and admit something. I sometimes have trouble making time to sit, get into an alpha state, and play with the sophisms. But, I will not let myself get stressed about it, because sometimes my most pleasant alpha states come from not doing anything "productive." If sitting quietly is not for you right now, find another way to be relaxed and engaged. As always, play with these sophisms and then give your subconscious time to assemble a good idea. Write down whatever gift your subconscious gives to you. Not only will you be surprised by what it delivers to you, you will be surprised by when it delivers it to you.

Exercise 26

MUSICAL NORM

"Music is what feelings sound like out loud."

Georgia Cates
From her book, *Beauty from Pain*

This is a great quote, though in truth, I know very little about who Georgia Cates is.

Learning to Play

When I was 24, I made myself take piano lessons. I remember trying to learn some rock covers in addition to some basic theory. Well, my trying to play was like a monkey jumping on a keyboard trying to type. Finally, my piano teacher, Norm, sat down and effortlessly played the '80s rock ballad that I was struggling with. I was amazed. Not just cognitively, but emotionally. By reading the sheet music as easily as you are reading this, Norm created music and feeling.

It was the true intersection of the material and form worlds (*see the previous exercise for more on the form and material worlds*). The tangible paper the music was written on and the observable behavior of pressing keys in a certain order produced something powerful, albeit abstract. As powerful as his effortlessly playing an emotional song he had never seen was, it can't be proven that the music or the emotion ever existed.

What Does This Have to Do with Helping People Reach Their Professional Goals and Have Revenue-Generating Ideas More Often?

SONG VS PROFIT

We're going to make the comparison between a song and profit. concepts are created from many other components working together. Even simple songs have melody, rhythm, and lyrics; even a businesses comprised of only one person has customers, product fulfillment, and expenses.

Understanding the Whole

My untrained musical ear did not understand how the components worked together. Of course, notes, sheet music, piano keys cannot think for themselves, but employees can. As a manager, you should know how the components of your business work together.

Two things

> **The first:** Ask yourself if your employees know what part of the "song" they are?

> **The second:** Reflect on the idea that songs can be improved when a component or two is tweaked.

Gestalt

There is a concept in psychology called Gestalt (pronounced *guh-'shtalt*). It refers to the idea that the whole is more than the sum of its parts[35]. This means that the song is more than the notes and sounds that comprise it, a business is more than its individual components, and a human is more than a bunch of organs working together.

The Whole Is Greater...
Think of Frankenstein's monster. (Frankenstein was the scientist; the iconic sewn-together, reanimated creature never had a name.) It had all of the body parts, but it wasn't human. What was missing? That's a pretty good sophism. Hopefully you can use that one as you sit and relax.

Will reflecting on the sophism of Frankenstein's monster give you an innovative idea right away? Maybe. But, this process isn't about the short term. No one can get in shape overnight. By regularly stretching and flexing your mind, creativity will flow.

So, for those who are reading this and can't seem to find their transformative idea, let me ask you what I asked about Frankenstein's monster:

What's missing?

Asking Is More Important than Getting an Answer
When I asked my piano teacher in wonderment, "How can you do that?" And I meant that in a very specific, literal way; I wanted to know each step so I could replicate it. He said he didn't know. He replied with a question and asking me how I could take a pattern of ink squiggles and form thoughts out of them. Just as you might not be able to answer what is missing from Frankenstein's monster, just as Norm couldn't answer what music is made of, it might be impossible to explain how the sophisms in this exercise can actually prompt someone to think creatively.

Too Much?
OK, OK, maybe the last few paragraphs got a bit too abstract. Maybe you're like me and want it broken down into specific steps so it can be replicated. This is the Creativity *Algorithm* after all. We'll get to some specific "how to"s in a bit, but let me call your attention back to those previous paragraphs. I think a lot of those abstract thoughts are great sophisms.

- If Frankenstein's monster has all of the parts of a person and could act with agency, why wasn't it (he?) human?

- What is music made of?

- What is the exact point at which reading happens? Notice that you will never know, because observing yourself reading will prevent the behavior you are trying to observe.

Take a Break

Let me tell you a quick story about a real scientist, not an imaginary one like Frankenstein, who made a monster by implanting a brain in a sewn-together corpse. The real scientist knew more about his specific domain than anyone. He was *the* expert in his field. But he got stuck. He had all the parts—the education, the drive, years of experience, support—but he got stuck. A lot. Something was missing. So, what did he do when he got stuck? He made music. He stopped working and played the violin.

Without revisiting the more abstract questions about the nature music, let me say that the important thing is that the scientist stopped working and started *playing*.

When you get stuck, stop working and start playing.

It's Alive!

Let's go back to Frankenstein's monster.

>What was the thing that he didn't have that prevented him from being human?

>What if it was only *your* opinion?

>What if the only place he wasn't human was in *your* mind?

>What if in *his* mind he was human?

I suggest that you will have as much progress determining whether Frankenstein's monster was a human as you will determining the point where reading or music exists.

Einstein? Really? Oh My

By the way, that scientist who got unstuck while playing music was Einstein. When he got stuck, he stopped stressing about his problem. He distracted himself with pleasant engagement. Playing music can bring on an alpha state. He repeatedly said that playing music helped him think. Of course, not consciously, though, even Einstein couldn't concentrate on two things at once.

While he was consciously playing music, his subconscious was hard at play assembling raw materials into ideas, just like a kid assembles Legos into a unique creation.

TAKEAWAY FOR THIS WEEK

> For this week, I'm going to recommend that you don't get into an alpha state. Instead, think about what song would be a good soundtrack to your next sales pitch to a particular client. If you are not in sales, think of a soundtrack that reflects the solution you are trying to find. If you *are* in sales, ask yourself which soundtrack your *client* would want as he or she hears the pitch. Remember, sales decisions, like a lot of decisions are made by the subconscious based on feeling.

Exercise 27

CONTROL ROOM

I wanted to start this exercise by asking you what your weirdest thought has been. Well, that question doesn't work for a couple of reasons.

    1. For one, weirdness is relative. Weird compared to what?

    2. My second objection is the mind-positive idea that different thoughts should be sought after and cultivated, not belittled.

There is huge overlap between a weird idea and a creative idea. In fact, if an idea falls within the normal range, can it even be creative? That's an interesting sophism.

If you picked this book up and started reading at this exercise, let me say that a sophism is a mental exercise or cognitive toy that should be engaged with when you are relaxed. Doing so often enough will invite innovative ideas.

Now that I've gotten that out of the way, let me tell you about a weird thought I had and the time I went to a hypnotherapist for no other reason than I was curious.

Curiosity might sound like a noble motivator. And it is—unless you're the proverbial cat, that is. But it wasn't just curiosity that drove me; I wanted something. I'm tempted say it was something weird, but, again, weirdness is relative. I wanted to see if I could take a thought from my imagination (**see Exercise 25, "Filling out Forms"**) and make it real. In a way, the ability to manifest a thought into reality is what the Creativity Algorithm is all about.

The Possible Adjacent

Growing up, I loved science-fiction. Specifically, I loved the books that were what I would call "possible adjacent." I'm talking about books where the barrier between fictional technology and our reality was small. Basically, books that made you think. A central theme of science fiction is a spaceship. I loved the idea of a spaceship with a control panel. It wasn't necessarily because of the lasers or weapons that are usually prominently featured. It was for the ability to control the ship, particularly when something went wrong. I just thought it was so cool that the ship's captain or engineer could divert power from one thing and use it to do another.

That's what I wanted to go to the hypnotist for. Could she hypnotize me into installing a working control panel in my mind? Something that might give me control over myself? Wouldn't it be cool to be able to turn off itching? Anxiety? Pain?

Control Isn't All It's Cracked Up to Be

Before I talk about how the session went, I think I should reflect upon what younger me wanted. I wanted control over myself by installing a control panel inside a control room in my mind. If you have been following the Creativity Algorithm for a while, you know that control over oneself isn't the goal. While it might seem tempting to be able to shut down anxiety, that isn't healthy in the long run. Many professional athletes are encouraged to ignore their pain and play through injury. That of course can make the injury worse. What we want is a working *relationship* with parts of ourselves. Not control.

The Hypnotheraputic Approach

Leading up to my appointment with the hypnotherapist, I was nervous. I knew nothing about it. I had visions of a swinging pocket watch. It turned out that the therapist was friendly and down-to-earth, and she explained what we would be doing. It was particularly interesting that she said "we." In an echo of what this exercise is about, she explained that she wasn't going to do anything *to* me; she was going to do it *with* me.

I explained why I came to see her. She said it was unusual, but since I took the initiative and it was my idea, she was optimistic. After we talked and she put me at ease, I sat in a recliner. She had me put on headphones that were connected to her microphone so that I could better hear her voice, even though she was sitting next to me. She did what I later learned was an "induction." Then to her credit, she was able to take my image of a control room and offer it back to me in a way that synced with my imagination. When we were done, she offered me a CD of our session so I could practice.

Did it work?

It depends on how we measure "work." Yes, I still feel itches. And I certainly get anxious and sometimes feel low. But in my frequent meditations/self-hypnosis sessions, I continue to use the control room imagery—even after decades. Of course, it has expanded. The control room now has a huge balcony with Adirondack chairs that overlook a blue ocean view. There is a comfortable bed there, too.

Here's a sophism for you to play with:

Would imagining yourself napping in a comfortable, safe place be relaxing? Could it be as good as letting your physical body nap?

OUCH!

For those of you who would like a more tangible example of that hypnosis session having "worked," please keep an eye out for an upcoming exercise that details the time I had oral surgery without chemical painkillers.

Here's a second sophism for this week:

if you could have a working control panel installed in your mind that had five buttons, what would the buttons do?

What Does This Have to Do with Helping People Reach Their Professional Goals and Have Revenue-Generating Ideas More Often?

Control Panel Config

For the sales managers reading this, let's imagine that you are sitting at a control panel for your department, division, or company, or perhaps a special one for when working with a client. What buttons would you want? What would you want your employees to do differently? What if, like in the example I used above, you would re-allocate resources from something else with the simple press of a button? Now, for one more layer, would all of those buttons be outward facing? Would they all be pointed towards changing employees or clients? Or could maybe one or two buttons be pointed inward, towards you?

TAKEAWAY FOR THIS WEEK

> Find some time—no, actually schedule some time—to envision a control panel in your mind. You don't have to sit on a couch. You can do it when you are walking, jogging, gardening, or any activity when you are relaxed and engaged. Imagine a "good idea button." Really imagine it. What shape? What color? Now, here is the important part: imagine the wires in the back of the button. Where do they go? To what part(s) of your mind? Write down, or better yet, sketch your ideas in your notebook.

Exercise 28:

CONTROL ROOM, PART II

Induction

In the previous exercise, I introduced the concept of installing a control room in your mind. When I imagine my control room, I start with a staircase leading down. This is a remnant of the many hypnotic inductions I've studied. Induction is a fancy name for the process of going into a trance[36]. A common device is on hypnotic inductions is a descending stairway. So, I imagine that, as I descend the stairway, I become progressively more relaxed. Sometimes I overlap the stairway down to my home office with the steps into a hot tub.

Once I get into my control room, which is a blend of home offices I have had over the years, I notice there are different sections. There are a pair of Adirondack chairs that sit on a balcony overlooking a white beach and blue ocean. There is a computer-based console with all manner of buttons and switches. There is a wall of pipes and valves that help me envision the ability to increase one aspect of myself and decrease another.

There is even a bed next to a stone fireplace for naps. This is where things get very meta and where I find some of my more challenging mental work. If the control room represents a level of your consciousness where rules are suspended and thoughts flow freely, why would I need to sleep there? I ask you, what would be the benefit of taking a nap in your subconscious? What would your dreams dream about? Can you control such dreams?

The Sandbox

For the computer-savvy readers, you'll know what a sandbox is. My understanding of a sandbox in the programming world is that it is a disconnected server where experimental programs can be created and tested away from any other networks. What if you imagined yourself in a subconscious safe space that you built? What if you then imagined yourself taking a nap in that safe space? What if you then imagined yourself dreaming while you are already in a dreamlike state?

That pushes the boundaries of what our minds can do. Here's why. It is a fact that 99.9% of the people in the world cannot think of two things at once[37]. There are very rare cases where a person has had an operation to separate the hemispheres of their brain. But unless that has happened to you, you cannot think of two things at once. So, thinking about what you would dream about while you are imagining yourself sleeping in your control room is a tough exercise. But it is that struggle with a tough, near-impossible sophism that flexes and stretches our minds so that, over time, our conscious mind can better receive innovative ideas from our subconscious.

To Have and to Hold

But that isn't the only sophism for this week's exercise. When I give talks about having innovative ideas to different groups at different events, I often embed envisioning exercises. For instance, put your hands up in front of you in a comfortable position. How would you hold a basketball? How about a bowl of soup? You can use one hand or two. How would you hold a hammer?

OK, now...

How would you hold a thought?

Did that cause you a bit of a mental stutter step? Good. That sliver of time right there was similar to the moment right before you had your last good idea, and it will be similar to the moment that happens before your next good idea. How do we have that sliver more often? How do we make it more than just a sliver of time?

Relaxed Engagement.

The mind needs to be relaxed and engaged, which is another way of describing an alpha state. It's likely the state you had when you envisioned the control room and when your subconscious tried to figure out how to hold a thought in your hands.

Now let's combine these sophisms. Let's imagine you are in a control room and you are holding a thought in your hands. Pause here. Stop reading for a bit and really envision the thought in your mind. How big is the thought in your imaginary hands? What is the texture? Color? What is the sound of a thought? How about the aroma? There are quite a few directions to go with this layered sophism.

I think it is a sign of creative strength that your subconscious easily imagined that a thought was physically in the hands of the you that was sitting in your safe space. It didn't consciously analyze or ask the logical question of the origin of the thought, and neither did it ask the *content* of the thought of the thought in your hands.

Let's Recap

You are sitting comfortably in your imaginary control room for your mind and body, coming to terms with the weight, texture, temperature, and sound of the thought in your hands. But those are all physical attributes. Don't you think it's more important to wonder about the *content* of the thought?

Maybe it is like a DVD or CD. You can see a disc, touch it, smell it, and taste it, but you can't experience it until you engage with it in the right way, with a player. So, how do we engage with the thought in your hands?

What Does This Have to Do with Helping People Reach Their Professional Goals and Have Revenue-Generating Ideas More Often?

Let's go back to some of the imagery and use it as a metaphor. Imagine an instance when you—that is, your conscious mind—is going down to visit your control room. But you can't clomp and stomp down the stairs. That's not how relaxation happens. Neither is such clomping and stomping the best way to approach your employees. What if we said the control room might be the employee's comfort zone?

Again, tread lightly;

> *your presence might disturb the very thing you are trying to engage with.*

Let's suggest an employee has a good idea in his or her hands, just as your subconscious self held such a thought a few paragraphs ago.

How are you going to engage with that employee?

How are you going to engage with that employee's thought(s)?

How are you going to engage with your own thoughts?

TAKEAWAY FOR THIS WEEK

> Whew! We have a lot to pick through this week. I suggest that maybe we shouldn't try to draw distinctions between weekly exercises. Perhaps you are still chewing on something from a previous exercise. Perhaps this week's ideas don't do it for you. It's your mind; I want you to feel free to think what, when, and how you want. Write down these three questions in your notebook.
> 1. What do I want to think about consciously?
> 2. What do I want my subconscious to play with?
> 3. What does my subconscious want to play with?
>
> You can try to answer them if you would like. But maybe it might be better to leave the questions unanswered for now. Give your subconscious time; you will be impressed by what it brings you.

Exercise 29

SLEEPING JERK

Sleeping is a difficult thing to study. It's kind of like whales. Both sleep and whales are difficult to study because of how hard it is to see them. Of the whales or sleeping people that we do see, we must ask if they are representative of all whales or all sleeping people.

For instance, when thinking about your sleep, you generally only notice the instances where something weird happens:

- You couldn't fall asleep;

- You went to bed and woke up what felt like five minutes later, with a whole night having passed;

- You woke up a 3 am, did your morning routine, got ready, and found out it was 3 am;

- You sleepwalked;

- You sleeptalked;

- You woke yourself up with a snore or snort;

- You got that weird leg kick or other jerky movement right as you transitioned to sleep, which is often called a sleep start or sleep jerk.

The list goes on and on. All of those are interesting, and to some extent unknown, phenomena. People often ask *why*. That's too easy of a question.

I think we should ask how.

Think like a Researcher.

How would you study such rare sleep events if you don't know when they are going to happen? Further, where would you study them? If you study them in the person's bedroom, there wouldn't be the necessary brain scanners and other monitoring machines. If you were to study someone in a controlled environment, then maybe the presence of those machines might affect their sleep pattern and ruin the things you are trying to study.

Sleep, the Great Unknown

Yes, sleep is one of the great unknowns. While psychologists know a lot of what happens between the sheets, they don't know what happens between the ears. Of course, by saying that, I was trying to use a clever turn of phrase. Of course, psychologists know quite a bit of what happens between the ears if we are talking about the *brain*. But, if we are talking about the *mind*—well, that's like trying to describe what an invisible person looks like.

Did you have to re-read that last sentence or did it make you do a mental stutter step? That amusement and relaxation you felt was just like the feeling you had right before your last good idea. By getting into that state more often, you will invite innovative ideas to arrive more often. Remember, increased sales—or whatever your goals might be—are only one good idea away.

Sleep and Brain Waves

Here are some things we do know. Most of us should be getting about eight hours of sleep. In those hopefully close to eight hours, we go through a repeating cycle of sleep stages. That jerk or leg kick happens at the transition between stages. The full cycle repeats about every 90 minutes[38].

Brain Cleaning?

One of the assumptions about the purpose of sleep is that it is when the brain cleans itself[39]. For the roughly 16 hours when it's awake, the brain is doing an uncountable number of things and using an uncountable number of synapses that encompass an uncountable number of neurons and glial cells. While all sleep stages are important, the stage in which we dream—the REM stage—is usually considered the most important. But that is a bit inaccurate and unfair. That's like saying one member of the band is the most important. While REM sleep is like the lead singer, all of the stages of sleep are necessary.

REM Sleep

REM sleep is when we have dreams, and it happens most frequently towards the morning. Even though the 90-minute sleep cycle, which includes periods of REM, starts as soon as we go to sleep at night, those early periods of REM are quite short. Throughout the night, those periods of REM get longer. So, if we were not under the hateful control of the dictatorial alarm clock, (sorry for the editorializing), we would have a long REM period right before we wake up. That time, that REM period right before we wake up, is a rich, fertile field where ideas grow[40].

Alpha-Delta Farming

Now let's briefly allow that field metaphor to lie fallow for a bit while we dip into brain waves and states of consciousness. As you are reading this, your brain is producing more beta waves than the other types. When you are deeply asleep, your brain is producing more delta waves. When you are dreaming, guess what brain waves dominate? Well, if you have been following the Creativity Algorithm, then you know it's alpha waves.

So, right before you wake up, provided you have slept sufficiently long, you will usually have a nice, long uninterrupted period of groovy, dreamy alpha waves. To go back to the rich, fertile field metaphor, this is when all kinds of thoughts sprout up. This is no well-kept farm with neat rows of crops. For most of us, it is an untouched jungle where nearly anything can grow.

Rows of Ideas

I don't think it is possible to organize the subconscious into neat rows of ideas, and if you tried, I think your mind would push back. Have you ever seen the movie "Avatar"? Remember the evil, over-structured corporation that attempts to master and control the beautiful untouched paradise for profit? I suggest that that's what it would be like trying to control your dream state. Yes, I am familiar with lucid dreaming, and I think that it is fascinating and generally healthy. But, notice that the goal of most lucid dreaming is to explore and experience. Just like in the movie "Avatar", things were fine when the scientists were just *exploring*; it was when they started *exploiting* when things got bad.

What Does This Have to Do with Helping People Reach Their Professional Goals and Have Revenue-Generating Ideas More Often?

HUSTLE CULTURE

Quite a bit. The first and most obvious level for managers is to honestly reflect on the hustle culture of your company. Do you encourage your employees to get a good night's sleep, or do you subtly encourage employees to come in early, stay late, and be available at all hours? Tired sales professionals can be compared to a dull saw, and dull saws do not do their jobs well. The second level is that, just as you encourage your employees to have strong relationships with their clients, you should have strong relationships with your employees. Per the distinction in the earlier paragraph, are you exploring your employee's abilities or exploiting them?

As Ye Sew Redux

Now that I have laid out disclaimers about not trying to control your dreaming alpha state, that doesn't mean you shouldn't *interact* with it or *play* with it. To go back to the field metaphor, one great way to interact with the field is to plant seeds. Plant the seeds of the innovative ideas you want to have and then see what pops up during REM sleep.

A lot of folks say that they do not dream during the night. They do. It's just that they are not aware of it any more than they are aware of the plants around them silently growing. Everyone dreams, every night[41]. In fact, everyone dreams several times every night. Just because you don't see the dreams doesn't mean they don't exist. Don't believe me? How many whales are in the oceans right now? What if we said each ocean is like a stage of sleep? Just as there are different sizes of oceans, there are different sizes of REM stages throughout the night. What if I continued with this metaphor and suggested that trying to count how many whales are constantly moving through the oceans is like trying to count dreams that oftentimes blend into each other.

Dreams of *Avatar*

In this exercise, I have talked about whales, dreams, and the movie "Avatar." Fun fact: did you know that the idea for the "Avatar" came to James Cameron *in a dream*? Maybe you did. But I am 100% sure that you didn't know that the idea for this exercise came to me as I was waiting in line for the Avatar ride in Disney World.

If you have been following the Creativity Algorithm, it shouldn't surprise you that the ideas for this exercise came to me while I was with my family and in an airconditioned environment after exercising by walking around an amusement park for hours. I had, at one point in my life, heard that little tidbit about James Cameron and "Avatar." Then, in a moment of relaxed engagement when alpha waves allowed for daydreaming, the idea for this exercise was assembled by my subconscious and popped into my conscious mind like a seedling ready to begin producing fruit.

Money-making ideas often happen when we are daydreaming, which is a type of relaxed engagement. And daydreaming and nighttime dreaming are much more similar than people think. To facilitate innovative ideas in both daydreaming and nighttime dreaming, we want to develop a practice of letting go of the day's stresses and letting our subconscious come out to play and explore. That is why we want to get into a groovy, relaxed alpha state during the day and play with mental puzzles called sophisms to invite a good idea.

TAKEAWAY FOR THIS WEEK

> Do an internet search for famous ideas that came as a result of a dream. Many good ideas are attributed to a lucky, random accident. But, I bet if we were to dig into those historical ideas, we'd see a pattern of preparation, previous knowledge, and relaxed engagement. So, for one week, every night, write down what you want to dream about. I bet you will dream about what you wrote down. Of course, that doesn't mean that you will *notice* that you dreamt about it. You might dream about it but not remember it. Still, maybe, just maybe, you will dream about it right before you wake up. Try it.

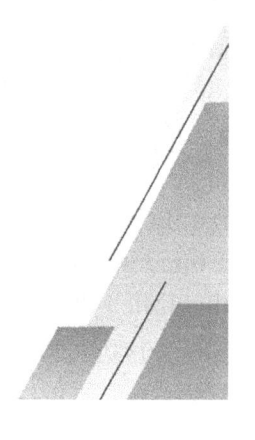

Exercise 30

MULCH BARRIER

It happened!
I watched an idea arrive. It wasn't smooth or automatic like I described in **Exercise 7("Thinking With Muscles")**. To be honest, I only noticed its arrival *after* my conscious mind looked away for a fraction of a second after I had been wondering why the good idea hadn't shown up yet. It was pretty cool to watch the good idea being delivered, and I am struggling for a metaphor to describe it.

For those who are new to the Creativity Algorithm, I have written about how a good idea is assembled by the subconscious and delivered to the conscious mind. That happens through a process of relaxed engagement. To recap, through some yet-to-be-explored processes, the subconscious will assemble bits of accumulated knowledge into a good idea. But that will usually only happen when certain criteria are met:

- There must be the right type and number of knowledge pieces in the subconscious;

- There should be an existing, good relationship between the subconscious mind and the conscious mind; and

- The conscious mind must be relaxed and engaged in a non-stressful task.

I had met all of the criteria. I had certainly read quite a bit about psychology, the mind, and creativity, so the first part about having deep knowledge was taken care of. As a life-long "imaginer," and as someone who has practiced self-hypnosis, I think I had the second part about a good relationship with my subconscious done. The third part was a slam dunk.

So why did it take so long?

I had spent the day doing yardwork, something I had done countless times. Specifically, I was mulching flower beds around the house. I could have paid someone to do it (there is the money-equivalent value of time to think about, after all; "time is money," as they say), but—call it tradition or stubbornness, or maybe I just couldn't overcome the inertia of doing it the same way every year—I did it myself. It was a beautiful day in May: low 70s, slight breeze, and no humidity. I had a total of 30 bags of mulch, and I wasn't in a hurry. I alternated between listening to an audiobook via headphones, blasting music via a portable speaker, and listening to nothing and just letting my mind wander. I was relaxed and I was engaged.

The only stressful thing I had throughout the day was that I was puzzled and disappointed that a good idea hadn't happened yet. I had actually been expecting one because I was planning to go into an hours-long, no-stress, mindless project; I was sure a good idea—or a few—would arrive.

After the morning turned to late afternoon, I still had…nothing. I was careful to gently shrug off my disappointment and redirect my thoughts to the possibility that the following day or the day after that were just as good as that day for a money-making idea to arrive. I knew that if I got frustrated or tried too hard, I would likely chase the good idea away.

Mulch Bag No. What?

I don't know if it was on mulch bag 25, 26, or 27, but as I was shoveling and scooping with my hands, I saw small weeds just getting started in their spring bloom. I didn't bother to pluck them. I just buried them in a few inches of mulch. As I did, I doubted myself. I worried that I was taking the easy way out by not plucking the weeds before I put the mulch down.

I knew I should have done it right, picked the weeds, and then spread the mulch. But I was tired and it was nearing the end of the mulch day.

As the green shoots disappeared under the blanket of mulch, I wondered if they would ever break through to see the light again. Bam! There it was, the idea for this chapter. I new I needed a new chapter, but the thoughts were not arriving - until I started thinking about weeds. The shoots were the idea and the mulch was my expectation, stress, or other unknown barrier. Would that simple metaphor have happened if I wasn't trying? Or did it happen because, for a second, I got distracted and thought about the weeds?

Clone Me!

Not for the first time in my life, I wish I had a clone. The obvious reason would be for one of me to do the mulching while the other of me got to do something more enjoyable. Mulching itself, however, much like any other home chore or work task, is not inherently unpleasant. In fact, once a person starts it, they often resist stopping and resent interruptions. In short, they have found a flow state[42] doing a task they originally thought they wouldn't enjoy. More on this in a future exercise. So, contrary to what might seem like an appealing idea, having a clone to do the "unappealing" work so that "you" could do the fun, innovative work might actually inhibit "you" from being innovative because you were doing fun work.

What Does This Have to Do with Helping People Reach Their Professional Goals and Have Revenue-Generating Ideas More Often?

Let's answer that with a question. If you are a manager, are you the mulch? Of course, you might think that your management style, techniques, and procedures are necessary to keep the pesky weeds of inefficiency from sprouting through. But are they inhibiting other desired growth? If you are an employee who is indignant and certain that if "they" would just listen to you, you could help the business, ask yourself how you are differentiating yourself from an unwanted "weed."

If that is too management-specific, let's pull back a little bit and explore the metaphor that the weeds are intrusive thoughts and that the mulch is one's conscious mind. The conscious mind's job is to try to keep the garden of the mind tidy, organized, and attractive.

So, you can see the quandary. Do we want an orderly, structured garden where we know in which row things are planted, what will bloom, and when it will bloom? Or do we want a garden that is full of surprises?

Obviously, this is a falsely binary choice. We can have both. We can have both simultaneously. (See **Exercise 9, "Defining Creativity**," for more in this.) Even if you, I, or anyone else wanted to have a perfectly manicured garden of a mind, a different part of our mind would rebel against such structure and confinement.

To continue the metaphor, Mother Nature does not like homogeneity. Every single person who has ever wanted a weed-free lawn or garden must contend with wind-blown seeds, squirrels burying nuts, and deer pooping out undigested seeds. Maybe, just maybe, for a brief moment in time, a lawn, garden, or mind could be completely blemish-free. But, to want that moment to continue would be to wish the stream of consciousness to freeze over. The mind is not made to be still.

Similarly, what if a person wanted a completely unrestrained mind, where ideas arrive like debris in a tornado? Well, we can see that such a chaotic extreme does not allow for ideas to be played with and developed.

Hesiod the Greek, and I quote
So, like the Greek poet Hesiod said,

"Moderation is best in all things."

Too much mulch or management will prevent new growth; too little mulch or management will create a garden that is out of control.

A good sophism:

Try to figure out how much mulch you need.

At first glance that might seem like an overly simplistic metaphorical question. Let's dig into it. (See what I did there?) Assume you had to mulch a certain number of gardens. How much mulch would you buy? Which process would you use to calculate that? Now that we have expanded the metaphor, let's ask what the gardens represent. Is one garden your family life? Did you want to block a certain number or type of recurring weeds from interfering with your family life? Is one garden your social life? Would too much mulch prevent new social opportunities? Get the idea?

TAKEAWAY FOR THIS WEEK

> As we saw earlier, we should be aware of oversimplified "either-or" questions. Though that shouldn't stop us from using them as conversation starters. Let's be more precise and nuanced for this takeaway. Let's assume different gardens need different amounts of mulch. After you get into a nice, groovy alpha state, reflect on the right amount of mulch for the various gardens in your life. As part of that reflection, plan strategies that will allow you to add more mulch, or even remove some, if need be. Writing down your plan will not guarantee it happens, but few unwritten plans ever get acted on.

Exercise 31

TEENAGE WINE

What does winemaking have in common with having an idea that will increase revenue? A lot. Let me tell you a story.

When I was 13, I tried to make wine. I followed the directions, or at least my barely-adolescent-self thought I did.

I halfheartedly washed out a plastic milk jug. I crushed grapes. I used some of my mom's sugar and some baker's yeast. Then I screwed the cap on and waited. I knew it would take some time. So, I waited, which is hard for a 13-year-old. But I can proudly say that I successfully waited 24 whole hours. Then I checked. No wine. So, I screwed the cap back on. Waited another 24 whole hours and checked again. I think I did this for two weeks.

Well, I'm no chemist, but I'm pretty sure that constantly opening it and exposing it to oxygen wasn't good for the fermentation process. I'm also no poet, so, I can't describe the unholy taste of rotten vinegar with traces of milk residue that I had to hold in my mouth and couldn't spit out because I didn't want my parents to smell it. Thinking on the few seconds it took me to run to the bathroom to spit it out still makes me shudder. Now you may be thinking why I would taste it. Didn't I notice that it had gone bad? Sure I had. But I was 13. So, I took a swig.

First sophism for this exercise, what would a good idea smell like? Second sophism would different ideas have different scents?

Following the Recipe

My point isn't that I am a bad winemaker or even a bad 13-year-old. The point is that I ruined the process by being too impatient and constantly checking on what I wanted. Getting a transformative idea is like making wine. Gather the right ingredients, follow the process, and leave it alone until it is ready.

The ingredients are a good relationship with your subconscious. It can become good and strengthened by playing with your subconscious. The way to do that is to regularly take time to relax and be engaged in something non-stressful. It's not enough to simply zone out in front of the TV after work because you're too tired to think. That's not engaged; that's exhausted. If you have read up to this point, I hope you have felt a bit of mental engagement from the sophisms. That's the type of engagement we're looking for.

My ill-fated wine-making attempt showed you how *not* to have a good idea. Transformational ideas don't follow the rules of other life or business goals: drive, hard work and short term goals. Those concepts don't get the subconscious to give you ideas any more than yelling at a puppy will get it to bring you a stick.

What Does This Have to Do with Helping People Reach Their Professional Goals and Have Revenue-Generating Ideas More Often?

I don't have to tell anyone reading that our culture, whether it is pop culture or business culture, is all about the "right now." Too many business professionals are held hostage by the fear of a down quarter rather than planning for long-term growth.

So, our task is to focus on the near term *and* the long term. A true vintner focuses on the immediate concerns of the health of the grapes as well as the long-term process of turning those grapes into wine. The pushback I get when I say things like this is that there are only so many hours in the day. Focusing on two processes and two goals just isn't possible.

As mentioned earlier in **Exercise 19 ("Is DWI Unsafe?"),** the human mind cannot concentrate on more than one thing at a time. But that refers to your *conscious* mind. Your subconscious mind is not only able to multitask, but multi-*think*. This is where the winemaking metaphor comes back.

The metaphor is also a good sophism. Put the ingredients of a revenue-increasing idea into the cask of your subconscious by thinking of the "what" of your long-term goals. Then let your subconscious ferment the "what" of your goal into the "how" of your goal.

Don't be the eager 13-year-old who constantly checks, worrying about when and whether the solution will come. Give your subconscious time; you will be amazed at what it grows and offers you. If that is too wishy-washy, then let's make this a bit more concrete. Find your notebook, set a timer for 5 minutes and *do not* wonder how you will know when an idea, like a fine wine, is ready. After the 5 minutes is up, feel free to inspect your ideas as a vintner might examine grapes.

Next sophism:

How many innovative ideas can your subconscious work on simultaneously?

That's a trick question, because if you were aware, it wouldn't be in the subconscious. Similar to the previous exercise, I am going to ask you to prove a negative. I want you to prove that your subconscious cannot think of an infinite number of things at the same time. That's a tough one.

TAKEAWAY FOR THIS WEEK

Get into a nice groovy alpha state, maybe even by having *one* glass of wine. More than one glass and you might have trouble concentrating. Alcohol can, of course, alter our consciousness; that's why people drink it. But there are better ways to do it. Both physical and cognitive exercise will do it. So, once you are in your alpha state, reward yourself with this task: continuing with the metaphor that innovative ideas are like wine, would all innovative idea wines taste the same? Would each idea have a subtle difference? Would work ideas be red wine and personal ideas be white wine? Draw a table in your notebook where one column is labeled white, one column is labeled red, one column is labeled sparkling, and so on. Underneath each column write down the type of ideas that would go under each heading.

Exercise 32

TOMATO CAGE

How often are you on your phone? Me? I am on it a lot. Too much? Maybe.

Screen time is not inherently bad. Like anything else, it needs to be qualified. Vacantly scrolling through the *same types* of posts and videos is probably a waste of time. Reading articles, watching videos, and listening to books/blogs to gather information that might one day become the basis of an innovative idea is a good use of screen time.

So, whether I am staring at my phone too much is debatable. What isn't debatable is that I do have it with me 99% of the time. That way, when I do have an "*aha moment*", or when a good idea decides to visit, I can whip out my phone and quickly type in my thought. Right now, I use a Google doc that has about a zillion links and notes. It's my "commonplace book." A commonplace book is a diary of sorts where thinkers of centuries past wrote down facts, references, areas to follow up on, and, of course, ideas.[43]

DEVONthink

There are modern apps that act as digital commonplace books. DEVONthink is a great example of this.[44] Which reminds me that I should migrate my Google doc to a platform that was designed for idea integration. If you have been writing your ideas in a notebook or back of this book, perhaps it is time to migrate also.

And that brings us to a sophism:

> *When will your set of ideas be ready to move to a different structure?*

Notice that the presumption is that your set of ideas should move. That means that the current structure for holding your ideas might not be the best solution anymore.

Just as a productive and over-producing tomato plant needs support and structure, so does an imaginative mind. If your immediate response is, "No, I've got it; I'm fine. I don't need a new structure for my thoughts", then I gently suggest that maybe you are not producing that many ideas. It is the heaviness of tomatoes (ideas) that creates the necessity for the structure.

What Does This Have to Do with Helping People Reach Their Professional Goals and Have Revenue-Generating Ideas More Often?

Is the organization you work for structured well enough to support its growth? Do the employees feel supported and comfortable enough to grow a good idea? Are they left to flounder with too much freedom so that their efforts are unfocused and wasted?

The idea for this exercise came from watching my daughters plant a few tomato plants. I resolutely stood far away and offered no advice. I think they planted too many too close to each other.

Too Many, Too Much?

Can a person have too many ideas? It depends. If the mind is left to grow unstructured, then, yes, they can have too many ideas. And maybe those ideas can be too close to each other in a way that restricts full growth. Moreover, the psychologist in me might suggest that a troubled mind might produce too many non-beneficial ideas. But the sophism remains, can a person have too many innovative ideas?

So, what if my daughters planted *too many* tomato plants? What if all those plants produce lots of tomatoes? What if that many plants produce so many that we cannot use them all? Would the tomatoes die on the vine or fall and rot on the ground? Probably. But I suggest that, at least in the idea-world—if not also the tomato-world—it wouldn't be a bad thing if there was overproduction.

For example, when I started writing this exercise, the tomato vine of thought grew in a few unexpected directions. I picked the tomatoes that were most ripe, wrote this exercise, and left the others on the vine. What will happen to the other ones? Maybe I'll pick it for the next exercise. Maybe it'll fall and decay to fertilize the plant. It will not be wasted.

Here is a fun sophism:

What happened to all the thoughts that you've had that you've forgotten about? Were they recycled?

TAKEAWAY FOR THIS WEEK

> There are quite a few thoughts in this exercise. In fact, I suggest that the tomato metaphor gave quite a bit of food for thought (sorry, couldn't resist). Find your way into a cozy alpha state and reflect on where forgotten, decaying thoughts go. Do they all go to the same place? Try to write out the lifecycle of thoughts: how they are grown, harvested, and recycled.

Exercise 33

NO MORE STEPS ON THE LADDER

Will there be a point when you or I can't have any more innovative ideas? That is a scary thought. That idea bothers me and probably you too.

Should it?
Like any good intellectual explorer, we should ask *why*?

> Why might we stop having innovative ideas?

> Is it because we are trying too hard?

Or have we gotten complacent, no longer seeking new, challenging ideas?

> Will we notice which good idea is our last?

> How would we notice it?

I am not trying to start an existential crisis or incite a panic that the end might be near. I'm merely offering an extension of the question of whether there is a limited number of innovative ideas we can have.

My, How Big Your Brain Is!
I read a cool article by Stephen Hayes. In it he does some nifty mathematical extrapolations from the idea that an average person knows about 46,000 words. All of those words have several meanings. More importantly, all of those words are connected to a certain number of other concepts or relations. From these and similar concepts, Hayes comes up with an unimaginably large number of thoughts that our minds can have. His estimate is that the average person can have 4.617×10^{67} thoughts.[45]

I am not suggesting that all of those thoughts are innovative ideas. Maybe only a small portion of them would be innovative ideas. But, if Hayes' number is so ridiculously large that it is functionally infinite, then we can use the concept that even a small part of infinity is still infinity. And that's a lot of innovative ideas.

Remember Those Neurons Floating Around?
That answer approached the question from a *cognitive* psychological approach. We can find a similar conclusion by following a *biological* approach. There are roughly 85 billion neurons in the human brain[46]. Each one of those neurons is connected to thousands of other neurons and they communicate with each other using approximately 200 neurotransmitters.[47] You can see where this is going.

A Glial Cell? What's That?
If that basic summary doesn't highlight the vastness of the human brain, then consider that for most of psychological history, the only brain cell that was considered was the neuron. Well, throw in another 900 billion glial cells that can communicate and now the number approaches one trillion. (Note: Glial cells were ignored for most of psychology's history because they do not produce electricity and were thus thought not to communicate. Also, almost all brain cancer is glial in nature, not neuronal, because neurons so rarely grow.[48]) With that many cells communicating across countless synapses with hundreds of neurotransmitters, the communication potential of the human brain is, like Hayes' number, functionally infinite. Again, that's a lot of innovative ideas.

All of that still doesn't answer the question of when or whether we will stop having innovative ideas. As the title suggests, what if you are climbing a cognitive ladder on a journey of growth and exploration when you suddenly find that there are no more steps? The rungs of the ladder of ideation just...stop.

This is where I am going to abandon the numbers and science of the earlier paragraphs and jump into some nerdy science-fiction and fantasy. I suggest that if we keep climbing, the rungs will magically appear right when we need them as long as we keep climbing. Momentum and intention are the only things required to make the next step appear. Climbing makes the ladder longer. Therefore, by continually climbing the ladder of innovation the next idea will appear in our consciousness as long as have the momentum of wonderment.

What Does This Have to Do with Helping People Reach Their Professional Goals and Have Revenue-Generating Ideas More Often?

SO MANY CONNECTIONS

Let's look further at the two approaches for estimating the potential for innovative ideas. The important thing in both approaches—the cognitive, where thoughts are counted, and the biological, where cells and chemical transmitters are counted—is that both approaches rest on the idea of connections. If we want innovative ideas, we must explore the concepts of connections. Connections between brain cells enable our thoughts and movements. A connection between words can turn into an idea. And connections between employees and clients are the basis for sales. The more connections we have, the more sales we will have.

Let's Do It!

Our task then is to make connections. We already know lots and lots of things. We have billions of brain cells that process the raw materials of thoughts. We just need our neurons and glial cells to put the raw material together in *new* ways. Newness is one pillar of creativity. Usefulness is another. (**See Exercise 10, "Academic Definition,"** for more on these pillars.)

I suggest that, whether in our minds or in our professional careers, connections—or at least the right kind of connections—will not be made when we are stressed. On a subconscious level, people are remarkably good at not wanting to connect with someone who is stressed or anxious. Rather, we gravitate towards people who are feeling good and are in the zone.

Before the takeaway for this exercise, here's a sophism:

Try to think of one thought, concept, or idea that cannot be connected to other thoughts.

Pause reading for a few minutes and try.

I'd bet that realizing that every thought you have ever had and every thought you could ever have must be connected to something else might is a new thought for you. I bet you felt amused and engaged. That feeling is just like the feeling you had right before your last good idea. By getting into that state more often, you will invite innovative ideas to arrive more often. Remember, increased sales—or whatever your goals might be—are only one good idea away.

Disconnected Thoughts

When I give talks or do trainings with sales teams, I often ask about disconnected thoughts. After the event, participants come up to me and say that it is just not possible to think about a thought that is not connected to any other thought. I reply, "Don't say it's not possible. Instead, say it's not possible *yet*."

Which is another sophism.

> *Can you imagine a benefit to having a completely isolated thought?*

TAKEAWAY FOR THIS WEEK

> Whether it's being still or being active, do what works for you to get into a relaxed alpha state. Hopefully by now you've played with the idea of cognitive connectedness. Now, let's go up one step on the ladder. Would there be a use for an idea that is totally disconnected from any other thought? Imagine a glass case floating in the air surrounded by a vacuum. In that case is an idea so pure that it has never known another thought. Can you think of a use for that? Jot down any uses you may think of. Or, sketch a ladder with yourself on it. How many rungs away is the idea that you have been searching for?

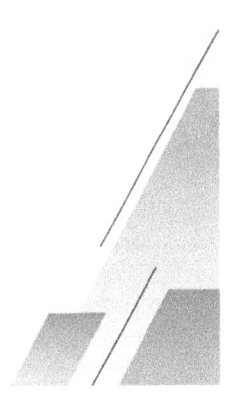

Exercise 34

WORD GAMES

Have you ever finished a New York Times crossword puzzle? Most people don't or can't. Newspaper crosswords puzzles are really difficult, but as I'm sure you know, difficulty is relative. I think the reason most people don't or can't finish a newspaper crossword is because they do not consistently practice the skills needed to do so.

Is the difficulty level based on the puzzle, on acquired skill, or on a person's intelligence? Maybe all three, but for this exercise, we're going talk a bit about intelligence. Of course, talking about intelligence is almost as difficult as talking about creativity.

Complicated Intelligence…Yes?

Intelligence is not merely complicated; I suggest it is *more than* complicated, even more than *extremely* complicated. It is perhaps more complicated and enigmatic than quantum mechanics. Side note, from the little I know, quantum physics, entanglement, and quantum theory are difficult concepts for many people, not just me. Notice how that proves my earlier point about difficulty: we're usually good at what we do regularly. Because I have not studied quantum mechanics, I can't explain it well. Similarly, because I haven't consistently worked at crosswords or played lots of puzzle games, I can't do them well.

Cubistic Dimensional Complexity

Back to the idea of complicated intelligence. J.P. Guilford, a psychologist who is known for many things, in addition to his theories on intelligence, created a three-dimensional cube model of intelligence[49]. Think of his model as a Rubik's cube, with each side being assigned a certain aspect of intelligence such that each smaller square within the larger side represented an intersection of those aspects. Sounds complicated, just like the concept of intelligence itself.

And yet I would say that Guilford's three-dimensional model is… not complicated enough. Here is what I propose, even though I don't really have a finished mental model of it: I think there should be a *four*-dimensional model, or maybe even a *five*-dimensional model, of intelligence. (See **Exercise 4, "5D Printer**," for a thought-provoking discussion of five-dimensional objects.)

I have difficulty imagining a four-dimensional model of anything, much less intelligence. Maybe it's because, like Wordle or Words With Friends, I haven't practiced it. I bet you can see what's coming.

This is a good sophism,

Imagine a four-dimensional model of intelligence.

Of course, creativity would be a part of the model, but how? That is quite a lofty sophism. At least for me anyway. Which brings me back to why I chose to write about crossword puzzles, Wordle, and other such games in the first place. The lack of practice makes them difficult for me. And that brings us to sophism number two: what is difficult for you to think about? Too many people, especially children, don't like math. Many people say they don't "get" poetry. Of course, like me and crosswords and Wordle, people stay away from what they are not good at.

The Importance of Practice

This exercise is not meant to be an overly positive, you-can-do it attempt to get you to push yourself to do what is tough. Although, as we know, discomfort is usually necessary for growth. Rather, I simply suggest that we should engage in Wordle, Sudoku, math problems, poetry, and other cognitive tasks. Here's why: I think that practicing puzzle games is a relatively easy way to feel the joy of an *"aha moment"*. Why else do you think people do them? By challenging themselves to the point of feeling that tiny mist of dopamine sprayed into their synapses when they receive the reward of an answer, they are making it easier for future solutions to arrive. In essence, they are training their brains to be solution-finding machines.

People do puzzles because they are good enough at the puzzles to frequently get the reward that comes with finding the right answers. That fraction of a second before the solution to the puzzle makes itself known is what is at the heart of the Creativity Algorithm. That minuscule moment where the subconscious hands the solution to the conscious is like a joyous baton hand-off in a mental relay. I think we should practice that. Not because we want to become good at *those* games, but because it is a low-stakes, low-stress way of observing, participating in, and feeling what many people know as the "aha" moment.

What Does This Have to Do with Helping People Reach Their Professional Goals and Have Revenue-Generating Ideas More Often?

Will working with puzzles help people have innovative ideas that will lead to more sales? Yes. Are there ways to get more sales without having innovative ideas? Yes. A current client could call out of the blue and triple their order. A chance encounter in a coffee shop could lead to a huge new client. But those are things that happen *to* a sales professional. If the sales professional wants to *do* something to get more sales, he needs to either do what he has always done, just work harder at it. Or, he needs to try something new. And which part of your mind do you think that new thing comes from?

Wordle Expert?

Could I become good at Wordle? Yes. Should I? Should you? Like any good psychologist, I am going to answer with the old classic: it depends. What is your goal? If you are reading this, it is presumed your goal is to have innovative ideas more often to increase sales or reach a goal. Just like, if you are doing lower back exercises, it is presumed that you want to improve in your sport or and mobility, not because you want people to admire your lower back.

How often should you practice unrelated word games instead of working with the problem you need a solution to? Let me answer that question with another question: how often should a basketball player work on strengthening her lower back muscles instead of working on a layup, jump shot, or other more overtly applicable skill?

TAKEAWAY FOR THIS WEEK

> Find a crossword puzzle. But make sure to find one that is easy (especially if you are new to them). Spend 15 minutes on it. You will find a few answers. Enjoy it when you do. The goal isn't to finish it, but to watch the mental process. When you are playing with that crossword have your notebook handy. Describe the feeling of receiving a solution from your subconscious. Then, give your subconscious time to assemble even more solutions. Not only will you be surprised by what it delivers to you, you will be surprised by when it delivers it to you.

Exercise 35

PADDLING TO SLEEP

Can't Sleep?
A lot of people don't sleep well. They either can't get to sleep or often wake up in the middle of the night and can't fall back to sleep.

Insomnia is a common problem. I don't presume to be a sleep expert, and I certainly am not offering medical, clinical, or therapeutic advice. Instead, I am simply exploring a thought and sharing that exploration here.

Don't Force It
In quite a few exercises so far, I have suggested that we cannot demand that a good idea appear any more than we can demand that a smart, skittish puppy fetch a thrown stick. The more we chase that puppy, the less likely it will play and return the stick. Of course, the more we chase after a good idea, the less likely our subconscious mind will assemble it and deliver it to us.

Just like that skittish puppy who kind-of wants to play but will only retrieve that stick when we are not focused on it, your subconscious mind usually delivers ideas when your conscious mind is relaxed, distracted, and engaged with another task. That mental state has been called an alpha state, a "flow" state, and being "in the zone."[50] [51]

Don't Try So Hard

Coming back to problems with sleeping, can I *gently* suggest that when a person cannot fall asleep or get back to sleep, they should *not* focus on trying to get back to sleep? I stress "gently" because my previous sentence is similar to telling a panicked person to relax. Again, this is a thought experiment, not clinical advice.

The Pesky Puppy Metaphor Revisited

To understand why to not try, let's go back to the puppy metaphor. Dogs might not always be smart, but they can be wily. They can read body language. They know when we are only pretending to not pay attention to them so that we can trick them into approaching. And our subconscious knows when we are only *pretending* to not try to fall asleep. For those people who find themselves counting sheep, practicing breathing, or doing other techniques to fall asleep, the inherent flaw is that they are *trying* to fall asleep. It's like trying to sneak up on an alert, skittish puppy.

If you want a puppy to play with you and bring you the stick of a good idea, the best way is to start playing another game—that is, without the intention of "getting" the puppy. Genuinely play the new game because it is interesting. Play it with your full attention. Then maybe, just maybe, the puppy will want to see what is so interesting. That is how innovative ideas often come to us, and it just might be a way to invite sleep.

Where Did The Paddling Analogy Come From?

The title of this exercise came to me as I was lying awake one morning. Well, sort of awake. I had woken up, went to the bathroom, and eagerly got back into bed. I was pretty sure I wouldn't fall back into a deep sleep, and I didn't want to. I wanted to hang out in that half-awake, half-asleep state where the brain produces a lot of alpha waves.

I couldn't get there. Maybe it was the over-eager expectation of getting there. Maybe it was *trying* to enter that state. So, instead, I thought about how our subconscious mind is like a slow-moving river and that our conscious mind is like a paddle boarder on that river. While the paddle boarder has some ability to move on the river, there are times when, no matter how hard they paddle, they can't get to where they think they should be.

So, there I was, back in bed early in the morning, an experienced mental practitioner and a supposed expert on creativity, and I wasn't getting into an alpha state. I was thinking about paddle boarding. That is, until… Duh, I *was* in the alpha state. I just didn't recognize it. In a multi-layered mental construct, I was in an alpha state, imagining that I was a paddle boarder on the river of my subconscious while trying to figure out why I couldn't paddle my way across the river to the alpha state.

What Does This Have to Do with Helping People Reach Their Professional Goals and Have Revenue-Generating Ideas More Often?

THE WHOLE IS BETTER THAN THE SUM OF ITS PARTS

If you are a manager, you must manage the whole person, not just the employee. There is behavior *and* personality. Trying to change an employee's personality through incentives alone is like trying to paddle against the current of their core self. You can't force change any more than you can force yourself to be asleep. However, once you get a feel for the employee's personality, needs, and quirks, you can work with them. If you can do this with sales professionals on your team, then maybe you can teach them to do it with clients. You can't force a client, but you can go with their flow and see where they will lead you.

Maybe, just maybe, this might apply to someone who has trouble falling asleep. When they are *trying* to sleep, they are trying to paddle in a direction that the river does not want them to go just yet. It is a biological fact that a person *will* eventually fall asleep. Don't believe me? Try to stay awake as long as you can. (Note: I'm not daring you to try this.) After enough time, you will fall asleep. I don't advocate pushing that limit. The same thing happens with trying to hold your breath. The biological need will eventually outweigh the psychological element of trying. Trust in that. Trust yourself.

So, if we know that we will fall asleep, or if we know that, metaphorically, we will end up on the other side of the river eventually and that paddling (i.e., trying to sleep) will not get us there, then what is left to do?

So...Stop paddling.

I know, I know, easier said than done. Especially if you find yourself mentally standing on a paddle board that doesn't seem to be going anywhere. You either want to paddle and try to get to sleep or you think that paddleboarding at that moment isn't fun and you want to get off it (i.e., get out of bed and stop trying.)

Well, what are we to do?

Stop paddling and start drifting.

Even if it is moving slowly, a river is always moving. William James, the founder of the American Psychology Association, coined the term "stream of consciousness[52]." Paddle boarders rarely paddle hard. They don't usually try to hurry the along. There is a time to paddle and a time to drift. Don't *try* to get to the other side. Allow yourself to float down the river. Let yourself see where the stream of consciousness of your mind is taking you.

The sophism in this exercise is to consciously help your subconscious get started. Sometimes our subconscious doesn't know how we want to play with it just as a young puppy might not understand how to play fetch at first. Consciously imagine that you are floating down a river on a paddleboard, kayak, or whatever vessel makes you comfortable. What you would like to find on the banks of the river as you drift down it? Maybe even make a mental list of a few things. Like pushing a kayak off the bank, it should only take a gentle nudge from your subconscious to start you floating. If it takes more than a nudge, maybe even more than a few repeated nudges, that's OK too. Eventually, you'll start floating. Who knows what you'll find? Give your subconscious time; you will be amazed at what it shows you.

TAKEAWAY FOR THIS WEEK

> Borrow from one of the themes of the previous exercise: we become good at what we practice. So, make time to practice this. Practice imagining what a perfect day, floating on the river would be like. Really push yourself to imagine the scene—the smell, feel, and sound of your time on the river. Practice enjoying the journey and not worrying about the destination. Maybe just a minute or two at your desk. Maybe even instead of getting frustrated while waiting at a stop light, you might think of what you would want to see when you try floating. Get good at drifting on the river of your subconscious. Eventually, you might learn to steer to where you want to be, but for now, enjoy just floating. Everything else, including sleep and innovative ideas, will come when your subconscious thinks it's the right time.

Exercise 36

WRITING A LETTER

Let's jump right in with a sophism. If you skipped to this exercise without reading the introduction or previous exercises, let me say that a sophism is a *relaxing, mental question that is designed to help you stretch and flex your mind.*

Here goes

> *What is the most complex thought you can have without words?*

Did your mind just do a little stutter step?

That is the magic of a sophism. It is a pleasantly weird question or mental exercise that can playfully shove your over-organized, conscious mind aside for just a bit. The weird feeling you just felt is very similar to the feeling you had right before your last good idea. By getting into that state more often, you will invite innovative ideas to arrive more often.

Remember

Increased sales—or whatever your goals might be—are only one good idea away.

Back to pondering that sophism, it is quite uncommon for people to be able to have complex, intricate thoughts without words.

What Does This Have to Do with Helping People Reach Their Professional Goals and Have Revenue-Generating Ideas More Often?

The easiest way to answer that is to simply look at what written communication is provided to and for employees. Is it easy to read? Is it open to interpretation? Too open?

Start Writing

The second and perhaps deeper way to answer this question is to ask your employees to write a letter to you. Maybe anonymous, maybe not. As mentioned in earlier exercises, the employees are like the subconscious of a business. What they know might not be obvious facts that can be written down. But what employees know might be even more valuable than well-documented facts. Wouldn't you want to read a letter from your subconscious? Similarly, shouldn't a manager want to read a letter from employees?

LEVELS OF LANGUAGE

As you may remember, the title of this exercise is "Writing a Letter." You may have noticed that I appreciate wordplay and cognitive misdirection. So that means that the title isn't directly related to the second step of having your employees write a letter. Give me a few paragraphs; then I'll reveal the main sophism of this exercise.

Just as we realize that thoughts are based on biological occurrences in the brain, we must realize that thoughts are also based on words. Even deeper, we must realize that words are based on letters, phonemes, and morphemes. Phonemes are units of sound (e.g., the "s" sound in "sound"). The English language has about 45 phonemes[53] (give or take, based on dialectal differences), which, when arranged and rearranged, can make thousands of words. When those words are re-arranged, they can make an infinite number of meaningful ideas. The Mandarin language has hundreds of phonemes. That, however, doesn't seem to have an effect on the ultimate number of meaningful ideas that can be formed.

Morphemes

Morphemes are units of meaning.[54] Take for instance the word "do": in addition to being a word, it is also a morpheme. It carries meaning on its own (i.e., "to make happen") and cannot be further broken down. That is, it is a complete unit of meaning. Now consider "re": while it cannot exist on its own as a word, it is a morpheme with its own complete meaning (i.e., "repeat, do again"). And now consider how these two morphemes can be combined into a new word, "redo", that carries meaning beyond that of either morpheme alone. That covers phonemes and morphemes which are basic units of language. Let's go even more basic—letters. The English language has only 26.

As discussed earlier (**See Exercise 33, "No More Steps on the Ladder**), it is estimated that people can have nearly an infinite number of thoughts. As this exercise points out, the huge number of thoughts people can have originate from a comparatively small number of letters and only a few thousand words. If thoughts come from words and letters and if a person would like to have more thoughts, they might rush to grab a dictionary or thesaurus.

What if instead of grabbing a thesaurus or dictionary as we talked about at the beginning of this exercise, the makers of such books reached out to you?

Here comes the sophism. They suggest that the English language needs another letter, and they have chosen you to envision it, design it, and implement it.

> *What letter would you come up with?*

Or, more specifically,

> *What letter would your subconscious deliver to you?*

- What would it look like?
- What sounds would the new letter make?
- Where would you insert it into the alphabet?

Will reflecting on a new letter in the alphabet give you an innovative idea right away? Maybe. But, this process isn't about the short term. No one can get in shape overnight.

> *By regularly stretching and flexing your mind, creativity will flow.*

TAKEAWAY FOR THIS WEEK

> This sophism pushes the boundaries of what I can envision. To put it another way, it is a tough workout for me. As such, I make myself come back to it regularly. I encourage you to do the same. Make time to get into an alpha state of consciousness. Then let your subconscious fetch several ideas regarding the new letter. If it brings you something you like, write it down. If you don't like what it brings you, write it down, then throw it back. Let your subconscious bring you another one.

Exercise 37

FAST-MOVING STREAM

When psychology was young—in fact when psychology was still unborn—there was a philosopher named William James. He is considered the first American psychologist and wrote the first psychology textbook[55]. James is quoted as saying something like, "The first psychology lecture I heard was the one I gave."

And with that, here's the first sophism:

> *How can someone write a textbook for an academic field that doesn't exist yet?*

James is also credited with coining the term "stream of consciousness." That simply means your mind is always flowing. Don't believe me? Time for the second sophism, and this one is going to require you to open your phone's stopwatch app and time yourself.

Ready?

Hit start on your stopwatch and try to think of nothing.

How long can you think of nothing? Let no thoughts enter your consciousness. Impossible, right?

It is interesting to note that there is a whole stream of meditational knowledge and practice that asks its practitioners to still the mind. People who practice that skill can have a still mind for quite some time.

Which leads to the third sophism:

Do you want to be able to slow or even stop the stream of thoughts? Or do you want to speed that stream up?

Whatever you choose, and hopefully you say both, will take practice. Let's remember that a theme of the Creativity Algorithm is to not try to *control* the mind, especially the subconscious mind. Rather we want to build not only a working relationship with, but, more importantly, a *playing* relationship.

Don't like that nebulous, namby-pamby, hippie talk? Want to get control, have a schedule, and master your mind? Gotcha. Before you try, let me challenge you to go outside. Go to your nearest stream or creek and try to speed it up.

And with that, here is the fourth sophism:

Where is upstream in your mind?

If we think about William James' stream of consciousness, where is upstream and downstream?

What Does This Have to Do with Helping People Reach Their Professional Goals and Have Revenue-Generating Ideas More Often?

Outflow and Inflow

Let's look at the information flow of your organization. Let's imagine that the employees are smaller streams. Are those employees' streams outflow or inflow? In typical hierarchical structures, employees' streams are the outflow. Information starts upstream from management and flows downward. But often it is the employees who are customer-facing. They have pools of knowledge about what works well and what doesn't. Perhaps smart managers should work on a way to periodically reverse the flow so that employee streams become temporary inflows.

The Greek philosopher Heraclitus is credited with the phrase, "*You can't put your foot in the same river twice.*"[56]

Which brings us back to the more modern philosopher and founder of American Psychology, William James, who, again, coined the idea of **stream of consciousness**. What is the beginning of the stream of consciousness? What is the end? Is the answer to both the subconscious?

If Heraclitus is right, that means we cannot put our foot in the same stream of consciousness twice. It means we cannot have the same thought twice. So here is the fifth sophism. You'll need a stopwatch again. This time set a timer for 45 seconds.

When you hit start, let your mind wander.
Stop when the alarm goes off.

Distract yourself with a dad joke such as this one:

> **Two fish were swimming up a stream. One of them hit his head on a wall and said to the other, "Dam!"**

Now, set the timer for 45 seconds again. When you hit start, try to have the exact same thoughts as the first time you did it before you read the joke. Bet you can't.

Here's Why

First, your brain was changed by the awful dad joke. On a microscopic, cellular level, it changed. Was it enough to prevent you from stepping in the exact same mental footsteps as your previous attempt? Maybe. Second, you were aware of the task and had some conscious awareness of what you were trying to do, and that conscious interference prevented you from truly letting your thoughts flow in the exact same way.

Now, before you start to argue and say that you can have the same thoughts twice, I suppose that's true for concepts like 2+2 is 4. Maybe. Remember to ask yourself if you are a good and impartial judge of your own thoughts? Also, remember that you are always changing, so it's never the same you.

To sum up,
Every thought you have changes your mind. Which, then changes the way you think of even familiar thoughts.

TAKEAWAY FOR THIS WEEK

> Make time for three alpha state sessions this week. Maybe take a walk, engage in your hobby, or work with some breathing exercises. How you get into that state is up to you. Once you do, imagine a grate or a filter stretched across a stream. It is designed to catch litter and impurities. If such a grate or filter was stretched across your stream of consciousness, what might it find? This is one heck of a sophism. Please use your notebook to jot down what things a filter or grate across your mental stream might catch.

Exercise 38

WRITER'S BLOCK

I wouldn't be surprised if, based on the title, this exercise is the one that many readers jump to. In addition to referencing a common struggle, the title is simple and straightforward. For nearly every other exercise, I tried to come up with a title that is catchy, off-beat, or a play on words.

This is self-explanatory, provided you know what writer's block is, but that's a narrow name. Writer's block should be relabeled more broadly—not as artist's block, but as creator's block. After all, not all artists are writers and not all creators are artists. An engineer can be a creator, an accountant can be a creator, and, of course, if you have been following the exercises in *The Creativity Algorithm*, then you know that business professionals can be creators.

If you have felt creator's block, here is a sophism,

What are you blocked from?

In a few paragraphs, I'll ask what you're blocked *by*. "Blocked" implies travel, and "travel" implies destination.

Where were you going?

Where do you want your ideas to go?

To others?

In previous exercises, the term "flow state" was introduced as another way to describe being in the creative zone[57]. Did you notice that flow is the exact opposite of blocked?

This book was assembled from blog posts. Of course, the blog posts had to be written, and that process isn't always smooth. So, in a self-fulfilling prophecy, I had writer's block as I was writing this exercise. I took a break from writing, waited a few days, and then restarted.

When I came back to it, I was reflecting on the idea that I should make a sophism out of encouraging readers to envision the block.

Is it rectangular?

Is it shaped like a wall or a brick?

What color is it?

Does it have a door through it?

Must we go around it?

Over it?

Under it?

Whatever initially popped into your mind at those preceding questions, it is a good sophism for you to elaborate on it.

Build on what you came up with. Add details. If you can imagine the metaphor, you can play with it.

Take control of what's in your mind. It is interesting that just having patients rate their pain on a scale of 1-10 often reduced their experience of discomfort.

Take Control How?
Before a person can take control of their mind, they should know what they are about to take control of. I don't think the conscious mind can *control* the subconscious any more than a human being on top of an elephant can control that powerful, independent-minded animal[58]. If you have been working with these exercises, then it might not surprise you that the subconscious mind will deliver weird little mental tidbits at unexpected times.

> *"You can't control your subconscious mind, but you can control your conscious thoughts, and through them, you can influence the direction of your subconscious mind."*
>
> — Unknown

Fixing Blockages
My writer's block was broken (if we think of it as a temporary blockage in the flow of creativity) when I remembered a quote from Socrates. I hadn't thought of that philosopher in decades.

Socrates
Socrates is arguably the most well-known philosopher. One of his key teachings is in the commandment: "Know thyself."[59] He believed that a person could not achieve true happiness or widom without understanding their own desires and motivations.

By definition, we cannot know our *subconscious*; if we did, it wouldn't be *sub*conscious anymore. Still, we might be able to learn more about our *relationship* with it.

What Does This Have to Do with Helping People Reach Their Professional Goals and Have Revenue-Generating Ideas More Often?

DRY SPELLS

All sales professionals hit blocks or dry spells. Often the problem is that those professionals are too close to their blockage. Consider the analogy of standing one inch away from a closed door. The door will fill up your whole field of vision. You will be unable to see that there might be another door or a window only a short distance away. Sales managers should help their team members conceptualize and analyze the blockage. Perhaps the blockage is an unlucky string of events. Perhaps the blockage is due to a predictable seasonal downturn. Or perhaps the blockage is internal.

The sophisms in *The Creativity Algorithm* are an attempt to get innovative ideas to arrive in the conscious mind more often. We do this by slowly examining our minds and by playing with the subconscious mind.

People Handler
A good sales manager is not simply a manager of sales professionals; he is a manager of people. A good sales manager can help his team members go around it, over it, or under it.

Mid-Term vs Long-Term
What if, just what if, we have it backward? What if getting innovative ideas to achieve more sales—or whatever other goal we desire—is the mid-term goal? What if the true, long-term goal is self-discovery, like Socrates said, and we should not be seeking innovative ideas as the ends but using them as the means? Now, if you knew as much as you could about the relationship with your subconscious and that relationship was

healthy and mutually supportive, wouldn't innovative ideas flow more freely? That is a good sophism.
What should you pursue first?

> **Money-making ideas or a good relationship with your subconscious?**

TAKEAWAY FOR THIS WEEK

> Draw a picture of your creator's block. If you are too scared to actually take a pencil and paper, (crayons are even better), then just search for an image of writer's block online. There are plenty. Take a few minutes and look through a lot of them. Then choose one that works for you. Now that you have an image, either found or created, take a few minutes, sit quietly, breathe deeply, and imagine that your mental picture of the block is changing in a way that will help ideas flow.

Exercise 39

THREE PAGES OF POWERING THROUGH

I've said it before and I'll say it again—routine is the busy person's way of getting a lot done. We only have 24 hours in a day. As mentioned before, sleep is critical to the creative process and for long-term health, so stealing an hour or two from our sleep time to accomplish everything on the list is not a viable long-term solution. How can we do our tasks and find time to invite innovative ideas?

Repetitive Recurrences

If we look at our tasks, we might find that most of them are recurring and repetitive. That is where routine comes in. Routines free our minds so we can look for new projects and challenges. That project can be *outside* of us, such as a new a more efficient way of prospecting for clients, or *inside*, such as searching for a new discovery in our own thoughts. This exploration would not happen if we had to constantly think of too many repetitive details. It also wouldn't happen if we were stressed about them. The thing with routine is that once you create it, you must follow it.

Practice Makes Progress

OK, now let me bring in the concept of The Morning Pages. It is a fantastic mental and creative exercise by the amazing Julia Cameron[60]. But it's more than an exercise; it's the foundation to the process of being more creative. It's a routine that Cameron insists that those who wish to be more creative do every morning.

When? Where? Why?

The Morning Pages consists of writing three pages, hand-written, of anything that comes to mind. What you write *about* is irrelevant. In fact, you shouldn't even read it or show it to others. When, where, and why you write it are the important elements. The when and where support the importance of the concept of routine; the why is based on something we have talked about quite a bit: that we need to form a relationship with our subconscious. Allowing your subconscious to freely hand your conscious mind enough to fill three pages every morning without a conscious censor goes a long way in repairing a relationship that many of us have damaged by years of refusing to play with it.

Cameron's book, *The Artist's Way*, is a masterpiece and a must-have for those who wish to start or wish to continue on their creative journey. In short, it is a way for those who want to be artists to work through their blocks and follow their artistic dreams. Cameron's idea, and one I happen to agree with wholeheartedly, is that we are *all* creative, that expressing creativity through art is *not* only a way to simply be psychologically healthy, but it is also a way to touch the Divine.

This brings us to a pretty cool sophism.

Is art created or discovered?

Many, many artists say that they are simply conduits through which God, inspiration, or a muse communicates. If that's true, does it mean that the art they make already existed and that as artists they simply needed to find it?

The amusement and relaxation you felt at the idea that an artist's creation existed before the artist was born was just like the feeling you had right before your last good idea. By getting into that state more often, you will invite innovative ideas to arrive more often. Remember, increased sales—or whatever your goals might be—are only one good idea away.

The Creativity Algorithm is quite a bit narrower than *The Artist's Way* in helping people increase their creative capacity. We focus on the process of applied creativity. The analogy I have used is that *The Creativity Algorithm* is like a coach who focuses on teaching a specific skill rather than trying to improve general athleticism.

What Does This Have to Do with Helping People Reach Their Professional Goals and Have Revenue-Generating Ideas More Often?

THE SALES PROFESSIONAL AS ARTIST

Before we get into specifics, let's agree that there is art in the sales profession. If it was completely routine and step-by-step, then anyone could do it. Successful professionals, whether in sales, accounting, or project management, must balance the art with routine. Of course, many professionals have routines to maintain the status quo. Those routines are for *now*. How should sales professionals, sales managers, and other managers routinize the things that lead to *future* growth for yourself and for your people?

For example, are mornings for follow-up calls and afternoons for prospecting emails? I am certainly not saying that you, as a sales manager, should try to make everyone do the same thing at the same time. I am saying that using routine to do repetitive tasks might allow your team a few minutes to find new ways to turn a prospect into a client or new ways to help the client increase their order.

Good Ideas with Less Effort?

As I mentioned, I am cautious with how I spend my time and cognitive effort. So Julia Cameron's ambitious program of fully freeing my inner artist just seems too much for me. I want a good idea with the least amount of effort. The Creativity Algorithm is just that—an efficient and pleasant way to have innovative ideas more often.

Let's add on to the sophism we mentioned a few paragraphs ago:

Is an artist a creator or an explorer?

Lewis and Clark, Stanley and Livingstone, and Dora and Boots did not create the things they found. Is it any different than with an artist?

The Universe and Active Creation

Let's keep going with this. If, as discussed above, artists are simply conduits that allow inspiration to flow through them to the page, canvas, or clay, then does that mean that all the art that is and that could ever be already exists? Or is the universe actively creating more things for artists to discover. I mean the universe is constantly expanding. If space is expanding into new space, will the universe find pre-existing concepts that it will share with a lucky few who we know as artists?

Next sophism:

Try to imagine a situation or example where improvement happened without routine practice. If you can imagine such a thing, what you imagined was the result of luck.

TAKEAWAY FOR THIS WEEK

> We need to find a way to make a routine out of playing with the precursors to good ideas. If you have been doing these exercises, you know that you need to get into a chill, engaged alpha state and be eager to play with your subconscious through sophisms. So, the takeaway is to write down a routine for doing this. Ironically, you must make a firm routine so that you will consistently have enough time to be flexible with your mental life.

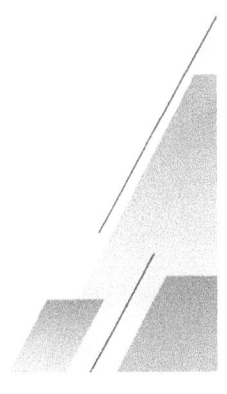

Exercise 40

MOWING THE LAWN

I'm not going to tell you how old I am. But I will tell you that I'm old enough to *not* mow my lawn. There's nothing necessitating that I be the one to do it, and I've saved a few pennies along the way, so I could easily hire someone.

So why do I, a man of my "distinguished" age, still mow my lawn? Even if I start in the morning, I am almost always sweating when I'm done.

My friends and neighbors think I'm nuts. They ask me if my time isn't more valuable and tell me that I don't know how much my time is worth.

Time is Money?

A few of those comments actually stung a bit. As a consultant who gives speeches or corporate training sessions, I had better know what my time is worth if I am going to charge my clients a fair fee. I think my friends and neighbors are looking out for me and are using shame and erroneous thinking as levers to get me to change my behavior.

Side Note: Shame and criticism rarely change behavior. I've witnessed their consistent failure on issues such as being overweight, smoking, or not exercising. The "shamer" might believe they're being helpful, thinking that tough love is necessary. Maybe sometimes it is. However, these tactics often hurt the person rather than help them. You wouldn't do surgery on your loved ones, so why would you attempt to give them therapy? Guess what happens when a person gets hurt: they lean on maladaptive coping mechanisms even more.

Back to Mowing the Lawn

Why do I do it? Let me answer that with a question: what would I replace it with? Being productive? Doing work from home? Getting stuff done? In the air conditioning? I bet you might be thinking, "Duh!"

Let me ask one more question. What do you think I'm thinking about when I am pushing the mower? Nothing, everything, anything.

The Sweet Spot

Mindlessly pushing the mower, like a lot of repetitive tasks, lets my subconscious come out to play. I'm free. No interruptions. An hour to myself. Just me and my thoughts. It's the sweet spot of zoning out and being in the zone. That sweet spot is where innovative ideas arrive. That's why I still mow my lawn. *Now*, how much is that time worth?

The point isn't to cut my grass or even get a bit of physical exercise. The point is to get mental exercise, to flex and stretch my mind. Let me ask you, when was the last time you took time to let your subconscious play? Hopefully, you're going to respond, "Last week," referring to when you tried the takeaway from last week's exercise. A lot of folks who have read some of my blog posts, heard me speak live, or heard some of the podcast episodes have said they love the content but just don't have time to do the exercises in the takeaways. I completely understand. Maybe there is some kind of motivational speaker or YouTube video that says something like, "Excuses are weakness," or "You'll make time if you want it bad enough."

Maybe

I find that those types of extreme motivational thoughts don't reflect reality. Don't believe me? Look at the stats for New Year's resolutions. In my opinion, New Year's resolutions fail because people don't plan for downtime.[61] They don't realize they have to recharge. That is why I still mow my own lawn. To be honest, and for a peek behind the curtain, I deleted a sentence from this paragraph and rewrote it. The deleted sentence was, "That is why I look forward to mowing my lawn every week."

I don't look forward to it any more than I look forward to a hard workout. They both are unpleasant and sometimes cross over into being truly sucky. Just because I don't look forward to them doesn't mean I don't enjoy them. That is not a contradiction; it simply demonstrates that the mind often makes up and follows its own rules.

I'm not saying that if you want a good idea, you should push a lawnmower around on a hot summer day. But ask yourself—when do you do your best thinking?

What Does This Have to Do with Helping People Reach Their Professional Goals and Have Revenue-Generating Ideas More Often?

THEORETICAL DOWNTIME

I think the importance of downtime is pretty obvious in a theoretical way. But the reality is that few of us have time for downtime.

So here is our first sophism:

Find a way to rethink downtime.

Don't just come up with a clever new label. Challenge yourself to think of downtime the same way you might think of investing in your 401k. What I mean by that is investing in retirement takes away a bit of resources now so that it can grow to more resources in the future. It is the same with taking time away from work now: so that you can do more work more efficiently in the future.

Cognitive Reframing

In psychology, we call that "cognitive reframing." Another example of cognitive reframing for the hard-driven, go-getters who sacrifice sleep for productivity is that healthy sleep habits will decrease the chance of losing productivity from getting sick. Going to bed early or sleeping in on weekends takes time away from what too many people think is valuable work time. Same with taking breaks throughout the day to play with your subconscious. Doing so seems to take time away from "being productive." Let me state an ironclad rule for healthy living. Your body requires rest, whether that's for sleep or to recover from an illness. How you spend that time in bed is up to you.

Which brings me back to mowing my lawn. It takes time but gives so much more in return.

TAKEAWAY FOR THIS WEEK

Remember how I asked you to rethink downtime? How about rethinking boredom. In our society, especially with social media, boredom has become something to be feared. The fear of boredom, like the fear of pain, has become worse than actually experiencing it. With that in mind, find time to sit quietly, slow your breathing, calm your mind, and let your conscious mind become so bored that it takes a break. Guess what will take its place? The subconscious. The longer you sit quietly, the more ideas your subconscious will bring you. Write them *all* down.

Exercise 41

DROPPING KIDS OFF AT CAMP

Did you go to summer camp? Did you love it or hate it? I bet you don't really know.

Our memories are not accurate and that is probably by design. One way to study psychology is from the evolutionary approach. We can say that nothing about the human species is by accident. We are not, as a rule, designed to encode things (encode is the fancy word for putting something into our minds) and retrieve (fancy word for getting something out of our minds) with any guarantee of accuracy.[62]

Mother Nature has decided that a memory that stores details like a computer was not necessary to our species' survival. The problem is that we usually don't *know* that our memories are inaccurate. Trying to determine whether our own memories are accurate is like trying to feel what the inside of our skin feels like.

Pile It On

When we encode a new piece of information, our mind/brain takes the incoming information and separates it into piles or categories. Let's use the example of a firetruck. When you encode seeing a firetruck, your mind takes that information and tears it apart into categories and puts them in pre-existing piles of information in your mind. Sirens go with sirens, hoses go with hoses, flashing lights go with flashing lights, and so on. So, when you want to retrieve a particular fire truck you have seen, your mind will assemble a memory from those piles: red, siren, hoses, and flashing lights. What you retrieved might not be exactly what you encoded, but it is close enough and you will not notice the difference.

With enough time and enough re-encoding and re-retrieving, the memory can become so inaccurate it is basically false.[63] Think of a song that has been played from a cassette player and picked up by another cassette player's microphone. If this is done enough, the song will become unrecognizable.

Which is why I don't remember if I liked summer camp. Was I homesick? Did I enjoy the summer activities? I would ask my mother, but she had four kids and would have even more false information to mix into the memories of one of her child's experiences.

Quick sophism

How would you know if any of memories in your mind, even your most cherished ones, are accurate?

The inspiration for this exercise came from an article I read about a mother who was anxious about leaving her child at summer camp[64]. She was concerned about her daughter being on her own. Was my mom emotionally ready? Probably. Knowing me, she likely couldn't wait to get a break.

What Does This Have to Do with Helping People Reach Their Professional Goals and Have Revenue-Generating Ideas More Often?

TRUST

Sometimes, the best managers, like over-involved moms, need to leave things alone. I am not recommending being negligent or leaving things to chance. This is about trusting the people who you have taught, guided, and mentored. Managers have to delegate and trust their people, even if it is really, really difficult to let go. That is for sales managers.

And More Trust
Now let's talk about sales professionals. What in the world does this woman's emotional turmoil have to do with improving sales techniques? Sometimes (more often than we'd like to admit), it is best to just let the client or potential client act on their own. A good sales professional will have laid out how they can help the client. After that, he should stop hovering. He should find something else to do. Occasional check-ins are necessary, but notice the word "occasional."

Then Find Something Else to Do
And notice the importance of finding something else to do. In Exercise 11 (**"Plant Another Garden"**), I used the idea that watching a plant will not make it bloom any faster. If slowly waiting for a plant to bloom is agony, then distract yourself. Plant another garden. By the time you are finished with the second garden, the plants in the first one will have bloomed.

A Word of Caution
The same is true with your subconscious. Don't try to be "fake" busy while really waiting for the subconscious. Be "real" busy. Be in-the-zone busy, alpha-state busy. Let your subconscious work on a solution or an idea for one problem while you focus on something else. How much more could be achieved if that mother dropped her kid off and focused on herself? The kid would be learning and growing, and the mom would be learning and growing.

"Worry is a waste of imagination."

—Walt Disney

Knowing It All

Let's go to the other side now. Would the mom be a better mom or a manager a better manager if they could read the thoughts of the daughter, camp counselor, or employees? Would it be good to know everything that is going on with another person? Would it be good to be able to rush in and solve a problem as soon as it entered someone else's mind? Doing so would never let that other person grow.

Here is another sophism for this week:

Would you want to live in a world where everyone could read each other's minds?

Will reflecting on that sophism give you an innovative idea right away? Maybe, but this process isn't about the short term. No one can get in shape overnight. By regularly stretching and flexing your mind, creativity will flow.

Disengagement

One of the major themes of the Creativity Algorithm is to disengage. As I say in one of my keynote talks, when you find yourself in a hole, stop digging. I know it's hard. I know we all want the next good idea as soon as possible, but we need to stop digging. Just like a parent should trust that their kid will do what they are supposed to do at camp, we should trust that our subconscious will do what it is supposed to do.

TAKEAWAY FOR THIS WEEK

> While I firmly believe that there is no "right" way to get into an alpha state, this time, try to do the method that is the most difficult for you. While relaxing should be relaxing, we all should increase the number of ways we can get into an alpha state. Or to put it another way, we shouldn't be limited to only one way to get into an alpha state. Once you get into an alpha state, reflect on the question of whether you would want to know what your subconscious is doing all the time? Write down your answer and any other stray thoughts that might wander into your mind. What if we said that just like stray animals can make the best additions to a family, stray thoughts can be the most transformative.

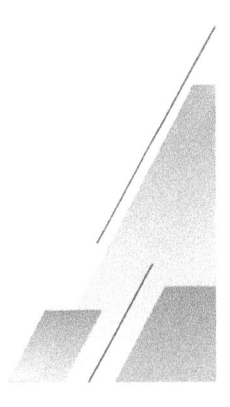

Exercise 42

SMOKE LEAF

If people skip ahead to certain exercises based on the titles of the exercises, I bet this is one of the ones that is most often rushed to. Obviously, these two words and the ideas they represent are connected in many people's minds, in either a tobacco way or in a marijuana way. Duh.

Connectivity

Let's talk about how concepts are connected. I think concept connection is a great analogy for neurological connection. If you've been reading these exercises, you know that I sometimes veer off and start explaining psychological concepts. Well, this exercise is no different. Here we go.

85,000,000,000

The brain has roughly 85 billion neurons. Imagine tiny little bushes with branches, a trunk, and a lot of roots. Imagine that each of the neuron's roots are connected to about 10,000 other neurons' branches[65]. The neurons talk to each other by sending chemicals from the roots to the next cell's branches. If 30,000 and 85 billion weren't already hard enough to fathom, now try to fathom 85 billion sets of 30,000 connections. Fathom it or not, that's how many neural connections we have.

Closing the Gap

Let me pivot away from science fact to science fiction. One of my favorite science-fiction stories is *A Wrinkle in Time*[66]. It's been decades since I read it, but one concept has stuck with me.

Let's Stay Neural

Before I get into it, let's continue to explore all those neural connections. Of the unfathomable number of neuralconnections, 80% exist in a thin layer that is more or less shrink-wrapped onto the top of the brain. That wrinkled outside part is called the cortex and is only a few millimeters thick[67]. Imagine four paper towels layered on top of each other. That is about the thickness of the cerebral cortex on the top/outside of the brain . (I say paper towels because, with a magnifying glass, you can easily see the fibers, which are a good model for neurons.)

Imagine one of the microscopic neurons in the cortex, which is on the top of the brain, trying to connect with something much deeper in the brain. It would be like you asking a friend to talk to a friend to pass a message to another friend until it finally gets to the person you actually want to talk to.

Easier Connectivity

What if there was an easier way of making that connection? What if instead of using that long chain of neurons, you could voluntarily think something with the neurons at the top of your brain and it would instantly trigger non-voluntary neurons at the base of your brain to slow your heartbeat without the message having to take a long journey from one part of the brain to the destination?

Back to *A Wrinkle In Time*

In the book, a character named Auntie suggests the idea of a tiny ant on the knuckle of one hand wanting to get to the person's other hand, which is a foot away. There is a string held between the two hands that the ant could use, like a tight rope, to walk from one hand to the other. What if the ant could somehow just bring the hands together, completely avoiding the journey across the long, difficult string? Wouldn't it be better to shorten the journey and walk from one hand to the other?

The Distance Between Two Points
Neurons cannot move in the brain, but no one said *ideas* can't. Imagine one idea that is far away from another idea. Normally, for an idea to get somewhere, it connects with a second, then a third, then a fourth, until, finally, it connects with the idea it really wants to connect and combine with. But what if that idea could simply move the hands together like Auntie's story in *A Wrinkle in Time*? What if that is how creativity works? Instead of traveling a long distance, an idea simply closes the distance?

What Does This Have to Do with Helping People Reach Their Professional Goals and Have Revenue-Generating Ideas More Often?

DISTANCE IDENTIFIED

How far away from becoming a client is an unknown prospect? How many steps? How far away is the CEO from the newest hire? If there is a chain to help those two people connect? Great. But how long is that chain? What if they could simply be brought together? Is it the best use of the CEO's time to hear the ideas of a new employee? Probably not. There might not be much a CEO could learn from a new hire, but could you think of a better professional development opportunity for the new hire than to spend time with the CEO?

Neurons change each other when they exchange certain molecules. Ideas change each other when they are brought together. And, of course, people change each other when they interact. Maybe we should shorten the distance between people in organizations.

Let's reconsider the title of this exercise: "Smoke Leaf."

Now, let's try a sophism.

Think of smoke and leaves.

Don't think of tobacco or marijuana. Don't think of a tree on fire or a leaf burning. Think of a leaf of paper. Think of a layer of smoke. How can a leaf of paper be connected to smoke without the concept of burning? Can you bring together those distant concepts without making a super long chain?

What if I said innovative ideas are created by closing the gap between previously unrelated ideas, like the ant in *A Wrinkle in Time*?

Sweet and Spine

Let's try another one: sweet and spines. Can you connect them? That's the second sophism. (Don't worry, the third sophism will not simply be two other unrelated words.) If you could connect sweet and spines, did it take a few steps? If so, that's OK. But of course, the goal is to actually move the ideas together rather than making a complex connection bridge between them.

Semantic Distance

Earlier in this exercise, I dipped into biopsychology to explain a bit about neurons in the brain. Let me now dip into cognitive psychology. In cognitive psychology, there is a concept called semantic distance[68]. It basically describes how far away certain ideas are from each other.

So, sophism number three is to think of two ideas that are very far away from each other. Before you begin, notice that you will probably think of nouns. Don't limit yourself. Use an adverb or a preposition. And for sophism number four, bring those ideas together. What if, just what if, you became quite skilled at thinking of ideas that were far away from each other and connecting those ideas? Then, think of your current professional situation and your professional goals. Give your subconscious time and wait for it to bring those two ideas together.

TAKEAWAY FOR THIS WEEK

> There is a bit of a chicken-and-egg situation with sophisms and alpha states. Working with breathing exercises and progressive relaxation techniques can help a person be relaxed enough to explore the sophism, and playing with the sophism can distract a person enough from their stressful thoughts that an alpha state just seems to happen. So, if you just can't seem to find time to sit and do some type of relaxation exercise, don't. Skip it. Just try to think of two or even three ideas that are really far apart. Write down those ideas on different sides of the paper. Do that several times this week. After each attempt, mentally walk away. Give your subconscious time to connect ideas that might seem far apart.

Exercise 43

UNCOVERING NAKED DAVID

I like to play with the titles of these exercises. Of course, they usually have a bit of misdirection, and this one might, too. Before we get too far into why this exercise is titled what it is, let's talk about art.

I have heard countless authors, artists, and philosophers suggest that the song, painting, sculpture, or other artistic creation existed well before for the creator "created" it. It's a wild concept to think that "The Mona Lisa" existed before DaVinci painted it. Even more wild to consider is whether circles exist before pi (π the mathematical constant) was extrapolated? Or, relatedly, how long did the concept of pi exist before Archimedes wrote it?

Those are some pretty darn good sophisms. I hope that those questions automatically prompt or even trigger a relaxation response.

It comes down to the question of whether you think knowledge is discovered or invented. The implications for either are staggering. If you say that knowledge exists prior to the thinker, then perhaps you are a believer in an all-knowing, all-powerful God, and must be all powerful, because knowledge is power. If you know everything, then you must know how to be all-powerful. But, if you are all-knowing, can you be surprised?

Here's a sophism that might be banned in certain religions:

Can God be surprised?

If there is an all-knowing God, then he must have already created all knowledge, right? Can you think of a flaw in that logic? If so, did that flaw already exist because an all-knowing God must have already thought of it? Did your answer just pop into your mind from the universe?

If all knowledge is *not* already created and is simply created as time and circumstances allow, then what is the raw material from which knowledge is created? We know that nothing comes from nothing.

If a good idea is something, then it must come from something, right?

As I am writing this, a lot of ideas are flowing. This exercise seems to be chock full of sophisms. Each sentence that I think is interesting, causes me to feel relaxed engagement, and that feeling allows the ideas to flow. I suggested above that ideas and knowledge must come from something. As another quick sophism, and using the concept of flow (both in terms of a flow state and in terms of the flow of the stream of consciousness),

Where do ideas or knowledge flow from?

Creative Discovery

I'm not a history expert, but I know there was a period of time in Western history called the Dark Ages—lasting roughly one thousand years from the fall of the Roman Empire to the Renaissance. During that time, there didn't seem to be much in the way of creative thinking. Around 1300, ideas again started to flow through Europe, specifically Italy. That's when the painting we discussed earlier, "The Mona Lisa," was created. Or was it discovered? Was the knowledge for that work of art, like the mathematical facts of addition or subtraction, waiting to be discovered? To help reconceptualize this, I am now going to substitute the word "discovered" for "uncovered." Knowledge, art, and ideas existed in Europe during the Dark ages; they were merely covered and waiting to be uncovered.

Michelangelo's David

Which brings me to another Renaissance work of art and the title of this exercise. The 17-foot-tall statue of David by Michelangelo is something I can't quite get my head around. It is nearly anatomically perfect and was carved without power tools, computer aided drafting, or even electric lighting. How did Michelangelo do that?

There is an anecdote that I heard about his process for creating it. When asked how he did it, Michelangelo said something to the effect that he simply *uncovered the statue from the rock that was covering it*[69]. That means that the statue was already inside the rock. He simply removed all of the rock that wasn't part of the statue. I hope that thought intrigues you and leads to relaxed engagement.

Let's use that concept for a sophism and for the exploration and invitation of our next good idea. What if I said that your next good idea is in your subconscious, already fully formed, but is just covered up by a lot of stuff? You simply need to free the innovative idea from what is covering it.

Creativity Defined

In the earlier exercises, I explored the definition of creativity. I tried to find the true form of creativity and give examples of creativity. Let's invert that. Let's use Michelangelo's method and try to figure out what is *not* part of creativity. Let's find all of those things that are not part of creativity and remove them. Then, we will have uncovered the definition of creativity.

What Does This Have to Do with Helping People Reach Their Professional Goals and Have Revenue-Generating Ideas More Often?

TO THE SALES PROFESSIONALS

Don't think of where your next lead will come from. Instead, think of all of the things that are covering up your next lead. Remove them. You don't have to create your next lead. It already exists; you just need to uncover it. Is that too simplistic? Did you roll your eyes? That's OK. That's your conscious, doubting mind talking. Let your subconscious mind play with this. Give it time; see what it uncovers.

TAKEAWAY FOR THIS WEEK

> What if I said the only difference between the Renaissance masters and us is that they didn't have as many distractions? Michelangelo might not have had a phone or computer to *help* him plan his sculpture, but he also didn't have a phone or computer to *distract* him. What if, just what if, our phones and our distractions are the things that cover up our next good idea? What if I said screen time was the thing that was covering up your next money-making idea? Write down whatever might be covering the solution you have been looking for. In a layered challenge, think about how the answer to what might be covering the sought-after solution must be uncovered too.

Distilling complex ideas into clear, coherent prose is an art form in itself.

Exercise 44

OFF-COURSE RUNNER

What are your feelings on jogging? A small percentage of people are devotees and love it. Most people have tried it and they probably feel like they should do it more often. I hate it. And I've tried, over and over again with all sorts of New Year's resolutions and promises to get in better shape.

Now, before I go down that road (see what I did there?) let's define what it means to be "in shape." This exercise will not turn into a physical fitness chapter. I would be the last person who should write such a thing, but we can use the body and physical exercise as a metaphor for the mind and its development.

Exercise Options

There are different exercise programs and different sports. Compare Simone Biles to LeBron James, or Michael Phelps to Serena Williams. Of those four, who is in the best shape? All of them are incredible athletes who have undergone training that is so grueling that most of us can't understand it. We are completely unaware of that grueling *process*. We only see the incredible *results* such peak athletes show us.

While we can imagine that top-tier athletes dream of results, such as victory, fame, and glory, we also must imagine that they do not shrink from the process. To reach stratospheric levels, champion athletes not only practice, but they practice practicing. They are students of the process.

Better Practice, Better Rewards

This is true with professional novelists, singers, and musicians as well. While I'm sure that many artists dream of fame, glory, and riches, the ones who reach the highest levels don't simply practice more than others; they practice *better* than others. It is interesting to note that when athletes and artists practice, they know immediately if they have reached their goal. Either the runner beat a certain time or he didn't. The musician either hit the right note or he didn't.

I am not sure such direct and immediate feedback is available for creative, mental practice. because the mind is unseen. It is often difficult or even impossible to see the effects of training. I have heard some people who have tried these exercises say that they don't feel any different. Others, of course, say they hadn't noticed anything until a good idea finally snuck up on them when they were least expecting it.

Regarding those people who have had an increase in money-making ideas, I believe they were so focused on practice and process that the results were inevitable. Regarding those who say they haven't seen any effects of this type of creative training, I wonder if they are too focused on the results.

Processed Focus

This brings me back to running and the title of the exercise. As I understand it, in the middle of a race, marathoners and ultramarathoners do not simply focus on a distant finish line; they often focus on the next step or their next breath. They are process focused.

Picture a marathon, one hour into the race. The runners are pushing hard. They are in their zone and in the moment. There are hundreds of people cheering them on. Those cheers are like compliments and validation. I bet such cheers and encouragement feel great to the tired runners.

But, despite how great the cheers and validation of the supporters must feel, why don't the runners run into the crowd of cheering people for even more accolades? Sure, compliments feel good, but for the runners, *running* is their reward, not the *compliments*. If they stop for the result of good feelings, they have stopped the process. They will neither have the process nor the result.

Based on that, here is a sophism:

When did you last seek a compliment?

That can be a tough question to ask yourself. Getting a compliment because you honestly followed a process and did a good thing is wonderful. Seeking a compliment by shortcutting the process is not.

Here is another sophism:

For what do you want to be complimented?

Is it for genetically determined traits such as beauty, height, or intelligence or is it for more cultivated traits such as kindness or diligence? What about accomplishments?

And here is a third sophism:

From whom do you want to get a compliment?

Knowing whom you want compliments from opens a pretty big window into the swirling, chaotic playground that is your subconscious.

What Does This Have to Do with Helping People Reach Their Professional Goals and Have Revenue-Generating Ideas More Often?

CLOSING THE DEAL

Clients know when someone is merely focused on the goal of closing the deal. Clients can feel that, and it doesn't feel good. No one wants to be used. Sales professionals need to focus on the relationship with their client to the exclusion of considering whether a deal will close. This is similar to how we should focus on playing with our subconscious without expecting a good idea in return. Similarly, bosses know when an employee focuses on a possible promotion only for the result of a new title and when an employee focuses on the process of adding value to an organization.

TAKEAWAY FOR THIS WEEK

> Forbid your subconscious from thinking about the feel-good result of relaxation. Instead, focus like a laser on the process of exhaling. Every time you think you are about to feel relaxed, refocus on exhaling. You can see what will eventually happen: you will become relaxed. You can't help but become relaxed if you practice the process of exhaling. The result will follow the process. Now, in a short few sentences, write down write down how many exhales it took you to notice that you were relaxed.

Exercise 45:

GOOD SORE

I have written about this exercise before. While nothing is absolute, including this sentence (*fun embedded sophism*), exercise being good for you is about as close to an absolute as possible.

Stop! Practice It
Before going any further, it's time to practice what we preach about exercise. If you are reading this exercise and have not gotten any exercise today, please read this exercise standing up or while doing wall-sits.

Back to a balanced life
That other-parts-of-life idea is a central theme in *The Creativity Algorithm*. Earlier in this book (**Exercise 3, "Gathering Legos"**), there is a metaphor of learning as Legos. The metaphor goes like this. *Playing with one Lego set is fun...for a while. But after some time, a person will have exhausted every possible combination of those Lego pieces. Adding a new set of pieces exponentially increases the creative possibilities.*

Small Changes, Great Rewards
Just as varying your exercise routine by mixing in different pieces can lead to better overall fitness, so does mixing in different activities into

your life. Too busy to take up gardening, needlepoint, welding, etc.? Aren't we all. Try this small change. Simply substitute a different genre of music for your normal listening during your morning commute. Change up the comforting sitcom reruns for a documentary or something from a different country. You get the idea.

Doing so stresses the mind just a bit. While I have heard that the word "moist" is one of the most hated words in the English language, I suggest the word "stress" takes the top spot. For this exercise, we are going to define stress as a change agent. Nothing can change without stress. Whether it is muscles, minds, or emotions, they only change because of stress.

The Creativity Algorithm is, of course, all about changing people's minds—not changing what they believe, but changing *the ability* of their minds. How do we do this? By gently stressing the mind with sophisms. I emphasize the word "gently" because sophisms are best *played* with when one is in an alpha state, not worked with as one might do with a task on a to do list.

Back to Physical Exercise

I hate the "before" of exercise. I hate getting up early, the warmup, and the impending discomfort. (Conversely, with ideas, I *love* the before of creativity: the relaxation, the playing with my mind, and the endless possibility.) But, I like the feeling I get after I'm done exercising. And it's not just the feeling of satisfaction; I actually like the feeling of soreness. Maybe you've heard the phrase "good sore" to describe the sense of accomplishment that comes with tired, aching muscles. The feeling of good soreness is a reminder that you purposely stressed yourself enough to encourage your body to adapt and change.

I want to know…

Is there is a good soreness
for mental exercises.

What Does This Have to Do with Helping People Reach Their Professional Goals and Have Revenue-Generating Ideas More Often?

STRESS RIGHT, STRESS WRONG

If sales professionals or any professional wants to change, there must be a bit of the right kind of stress. And it's probably not a manager haranguing them. It needs to be the right *type* and the right *amount* of stress.

With that, here is a sophism

> *Who should be the judge of the right amount of stress an employee is under?*

I'm always fascinated by physical therapists who push, prod, and stretch other people's injured body parts. How do they know their patient can take a bit more even when the patient says it's too much? If you are a manager, should you have the final say in what is too much stress for a member of your team?

Positive Change
The Creativity Algorithm is about engaging in pleasant mental stress to effect a change. How do we know if it works? Well, we can count innovative ideas. As we know, innovative ideas come from the subconscious. The subconscious doesn't actually care about our schedules. Trying to count the innovative ideas of someone who just started *The Creativity Algorithm* is like measuring fitness by counting pull-ups of someone who just started their physical fitness journey.

A person can end a workout without having done a sit-up, pull-up, or push-up and still have that good sore feeling of accomplishment.

So, here's our sophism for this week

Can you ever be sore from imagining?

We know the neural tissue of the brain doesn't have pain receptors. This is why people can undergo brain surgery while they are awake. But does the *mind* have pain receptors?

TAKEAWAY FOR THIS WEEK

> This week, don't just find a few minutes to get into a groovy alpha state and gently ponder sophism. Nope. Instead, cue the Rocky music and push yourself to the limit. Find an *hour!* Get relaxed, get into the zone, and THINK. About what?
>
> Here are a few fun sophisms:
>
> - Does nothing exist?
> - Is trying to force creativity like pushing with a rope or like pulling water from a fountain.

Exercise 46

ZOOMIES

Have you ever heard the word "Zoomies?" If you are a dog owner, you probably have. If you don't know the word, it refers to the mad dashing of a happy dog that is racing around with no apparent plan[70]. I don't think too many people could watch a dog doing zoomies and not break into a smile.

One day, I was doing some yardwork. My dog must have realized that I was outside without him and bolted out of the doggie door like a brown streak of chaos. He then put on a masterclass of zoomies. He would streak towards me at a zillion miles per hour, charging the lawnmower, and then veer off just as I made a fake move to grab him. He would dive bomb the mower—run in, bark at it, dash off, repeat. We did this for quite some time. I was entranced and loved watching his pure, silly joy.

Then it hit me, but before I tell you *what*, let me tell you *why* I think it hit me. I was relaxed, my mind was not occupied by stressful stimuli, and I was doing a low-mental-impact physical task. In short, I had created a great alpha state.

Human Zoomies

What hit me while I was watching my dog zigzag at top speed, really pushing himself, was the question of how we might get our minds to do zoomies.

How do we let our subconscious minds run free with such carefree energy? That is a heck of a sophism.

What Does This Have to Do with Helping People Reach Their Professional Goals and Have Revenue-Generating Ideas More Often?

OPPORTUNITY TO ZOOM

In my talks with management and sales professionals, I often challenge them with the question of whether they're giving their team enough opportunities to run, creatively run, that is. When I keep my dog safely next to me on a walk, I never get to see him really run, to see how fast he could go when allowed to reach his full potential.

Do you allow or encourage your team to impress you by going all out? If you say they haven't impressed you yet, are you holding them too close? Are they hampered by rules and procedures?

Going back to a dog running at full speed for the pure joy of it—imagine that such a dog was running towards the horizon with blind faith he could get there. If your potential were a horizon or if your employees' potential were a horizon, *how would you journey beyond it?* That is a great sophism.

Another question I ask folks who attend my talks or trainings is this: *"If you are not giving your subconscious the right raw material, why would it return the finished product of a good idea?"*

And that leads into the last sophism:

What raw materials are you giving your subconscious? How can it create a good idea if it doesn't have what it needs?

TAKEAWAY FOR THIS WEEK

> Try to find—or even better, create—a situation where you are physically active but not mentally engaged. Resist the temptation to put in headphones. Carve out time to let your mind run free. It might seem boring at first. Keep going. If your mind isn't ever free and unburdened, when will it have time to race towards the horizon and assemble a good idea? Just as you might imagine the zig-zagging path of an excited dog, watch, enjoy, and then write down the path that your mind takes as you let it run free.

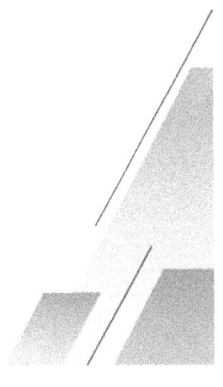

Exercise 47

FLOODED CARBURETOR

I have written before about how I value spending an hour cutting the grass just so I can have some time to let my mind wander. While I don't mind walking behind a self-propelled lawnmower, I hate weed whacking!

The machine is finicky. There is a little rubber bulb that you need to push a few times to get the fuel mix into the carburetor before you attempt to pull the string. Because the machine doesn't start on the first, second or tenth pull, I push the little bulb a few more times. In my frustration, I always seem to over push the bulb thereby flooding the carburetor and ensuring the engine will definitely not start.

What Does This Have to Do with Helping People Reach Their Professional Goals and Have Revenue-Generating Ideas More Often?

STARTING THE METAPHORICAL CARBURETOR

The short answer is a question. Has anyone, perhaps a boss, coworker, or needy client flooded your metaphorical carburetor? Have you flooded someone else's? Revisit the phrase: "You think like you feel." How do the sales professionals on your team feel? Desperate? Rushed? If so, are they hitting the fuel priming bulb too often? Are you doing it with them, for them, or to them? I don't want to finish the metaphor for you, but let's take a few more steps forward. Are you pushing them to reach their goals just like I was pushing too much fuel into the carburetor? Are they pushing their clients too hard and flooding the relationship?

You think as you feel.
That can't be ignored. Don't believe me? Right now, think of something amazingly funny. It's tough. (*Note: it is easier to think of negative things because that is how humans are wired. Evolution has designed us to survive by being worried, scared, and mad.*) However, when you are with your friends and family and something funny happens, I bet you can easily think of something else that is funny. That often results in a laughter chain reaction because, again, we think as we feel. Thus, as you can imagine, it's difficult to come up with a good idea if you are experiencing negative emotions.

Mental Set
So how are you going to help your team or help yourself think of solutions? First, you must do a check of your mental set (Mental set is a psychology lingo for what you are thinking and feeling)[71]. Doing such a check is another way of practicing mindfulness.

Quick sophism

*Can you or anyone on your team shift
someone else's mental set?*

If so, that brings up a whole host of other sophisms.

Evolution Allusion

Let's revisit the evolution stuff I alluded to earlier. While Mother Nature engineers us towards negative emotions, there is a hardwired way to jump-start some good feelings, which will, in turn, hopefully jump-start some creative thinking. I wish starting my weed whacker were that easy.

Laughter

Here's how to jump-start a positive mental set. Put this book down and go to YouTube and search "baby laughing compilation." Watch a video for a few minutes then come back to this exercise. Mother Nature has engineered a baby's laugh to be one of the best sounds we could ever possibly hear. Babies only laugh when they are fed, rested, dry, secure, and pain-free. In short, babies' laughter is a reward for good parenting. We can use it to jump-start a good feeling.

Once we have that good feeling, we're ready to play with a sophism. Any one sophism might not spur a good idea any more than one time listening to a baby's laugh will make a good mood happen. It will increase the *likelihood* and, the more often we do it, the more likely we will have a good idea.

So here are two sophisms:

> *If a weed whacker could trim away thoughts, what would you choose to clear?*

> *If your mental carburetor is flooded with too many stressful and non-creative thoughts, how would you clear it to allow the spark plug of innovation to ignite the creative mixture?*

Mindfulness

Let's talk a bit about mindfulness here since we skipped over it earlier. It is a broad concept that can't be perfectly defined any more than art or creativity can be defined. Think about the first part of the word "mindfulness": "mind." The mind is different for each person. We can describe it, even if we can't define it. Mindfulness is a type of meditation where a person quietly reflects on what they are thinking and feeling. Mindfulness can overlap with the concept of an alpha state, but I believe an alpha state is more active.

TAKEAWAY FOR THIS WEEK

After reading this exercise, I encourage you to be mindful of whether you are flooding your mental carburetor. Jot down whether you might be *flooding* your carburetor or if you might be *limiting* the flow your mental fuel. Of course, if you pick the second choice, you will have to define what mental fuel means to you.

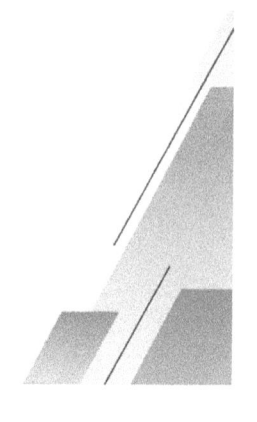

Exercise 48

HANDFUL OF SAND

Measurement Impossibilities?
What if I said that *some things are impossible to measure*? That is the first sophism

> *Think of something that cannot be measured.*

You might think of friendship. Well, I think that can be measured. Think of a friend. Imagine that you call that friend. No answer, no return call. You text them. Nothing comes back. You try again. Nothing. How many times would you keep trying until you stop? Whatever that number is, it is a measurement of the strength of that friendship.

Measurement Possibility?
If I say everything can be measured, that is an absolute. I'm sure you know that finding just one thing that can't be measured disproves such an absolute statement. Let's scale that back and say that lots of things can't be measured. Notice that the term "lots" is not very well defined. That brings us back to the sophism of *thinking of something that can't be measured*. Whatever you thought of…is the inability to measure it due to

a trait of that thing *or* is the inability due to your lack of imagination or knowledge?

Let's do an envisioning exercise and talk about the title of this exercise.

How much sand is in a handful of sand?

To do that, we would have to define a handful. First, not everyone has the same size of hands. Second, holding your hand palm up while someone piles sand on it, does not make it a handful; that's just a pile on your palm. To be a handful, there must be some sort of closed fingers.

Two more things with this idea.

> **First**, if your fingers are fully closed, then there is no way to count how much sand is in your hand.
>
> **Second**, and more interestingly, as you close your hand around the sand to create a stable handful, more and more sand will probably fall out.

The tighter the hand closes, the more precise we can be regarding how many grains of sand are in the hand, but if it closes too much, the amount left in the hand is too small to be considered a handful anymore (and the fingers would obscure the measurement process).

What Does This Have to Do with Helping People Reach Their Professional Goals and Have Revenue-Generating Ideas More Often?

WHAT GETS MEASURED GETS DONE

Have you ever heard that corporate phrase? Revenue and sales can be counted. Those come from employees, just as innovative ideas come from the subconscious. How can you measure the likelihood that a highly productive employee will *continue* being highly productive? The process of measuring can change the very thing we are trying to measure.

Progress?
Notice that we haven't really gotten anywhere with this exercise. I correlate that lack of progress to the decades-long debate about intelligence tests. There have been some amazing discussions about the definition of intelligence and how to measure it. As deep and interesting as discussions about the definition of intelligence might be, those high-level talks don't seem to actually help anyone with anything.

With that, here's the next sophism

Think of a good use for an intelligence test.

If you think about it, finding a good use for an intelligence test is only slightly more valuable than finding a good use for a test for measuring handfuls of sand.

So...
If measuring a handful of sand is pointless, why is an exercise in this book dedicated to it?

Because sophisms and rhetorical questions are designed to flex and stretch the mind so that the next time you need your mind to reach beyond itself, it will be more comfortable doing so.

Let's use the task of *counting something pointless* as a sophism for this week. Do you blink more often than you breathe? Do you realize that by attempting to count such things, you have become conscious of them? Becoming conscious of them, of course, changes their nature and makes it impossible to get an accurate count? Did that question distract you just enough for your subconscious mind to peek out and say, "*Gee, that's interesting*"?

That's what we want.

We want the subconscious to come out and play, because when it does, it brings good ideas.

TAKEAWAY FOR THIS WEEK

I can't imagine any kid in an elementary school who thinks of defining vocabulary words as play. But, since we're not in elementary school, we are going to play with definitions. Use your journal and write down a list of five things that cannot be defined or measured. Your conscious mind should come up with the list. You know what else your conscious mind should do? It should *forbid* your subconscious mind from defining them. Your conscious mind should lay down the law and say that absolutely, under no circumstances, should your subconscious find a way to define and measure what was written on the list. I bet you can predict what will happen. Next step, forbid your subconscious mind from defining a path towards your goals.

Exercise 49

SWEET RELEASE

Priming
Let's jump right into a psychology lesson first and then talk about some of the weird and possibly provocative thoughts you had when you read the title. Didn't have any provocative thoughts? Are you trying not to think of them? The fact that thoughts can be pointed in a certain direction is called "*priming*.[72]"

Priming is a powerful and subconscious phenomenon where an external stimulus or internal thought can activate a particular thought or emotion in the brain[73]. Advertisers do this. I know for a fact that McDonald's food is not healthy. I still like the commercials and jingles. Brand names and advertising campaigns prime you to trigger good thoughts and emotions.

Positive vs Negative Priming
The Creativity Algorithm serves to routinely prime ourselves to find the alpha state of relaxed engagements. Sadly, the opposite is usually the case: it is much easier to prime ourselves into a negative thought or emotion network. It is not my intent to be a Debbie Downer[74] or to offer therapy, but drawing from what I know of cognitive-behavioral therapy, the first step is to be mindful of the trigger and the oft-associated automatic

response.

Dominos Falling

You know what's an indication that I talk too much? That wasn't even the psychology lesson. But as soon as I thought a certain thought, that primed a whole cascade of thoughts about priming, which streamed into my mind from my subconscious like an artful pattern of dominos falling.

Negative/Positive Reinforcement

What the psychology lesson is really about is the idea of negative reinforcement. Speaking of triggers and automatic responses, I have taught this concept so often over the decades that I immediately hear myself repeating the phrase, "*Negative reinforcement is not punishment.*"

Negative reinforcement is *removing* something unpleasant after a good behavior is done[75]. Positive reinforcement (reward) is *adding* something pleasant after a good behavior is done[76]. That is, both negative and positive reinforcement attempt to promote a desired behavior.

- The stress of having to do a task goes away when the task is completed.

- The uncomfortable feeling of having to pee goes away when a person urinates.

Endorphins Make You Happy?

If you think about it, we often talk about endorphins as a reward for a good workout[77]. For many of us, it is the feeling that we got when the workout was *over* that is the true reward. The feeling of putting something unpleasant behind us is negative reinforcement. To repeat, *negative reinforcement is a pleasant consequence of having something unpleasant go away after a good behavior is done.*

What Does This Have to Do with Helping People Reach Their Professional Goals and Have Revenue-Generating Ideas More Often?

MOTIVATIONAL REWARDS

Many commission schedules are based on rewards. If an employee does x, then they earn y. But what if we came at this from the direction of negative reinforcement? What if the commission schedule was that if an employee does x, then z gets removed (z being a stressor or unpleasant task)? Think about the unpleasant thing that goes along with having to do our jobs. There are often a lot of them. Would *removing* some unpleasantness be more valuable than *adding* things that are considered pleasant?

That brings us to our first sophism.

> *Mentally make a list of three pleasant things that you would like to add (reward) for doing good behavior.*

Then...

> *Mentally make a list of three unpleasant things that you would like to subtract (negative reinforcement) for doing good behavior.*

That's the first part of the sophism. The second part is to ask yourself

> *Which list of three do you prefer.*

There are two things with this sophism.

> **The first** is the idea that reflecting on something like this will help foster an alpha state. And the more often we get into an alpha state, the more often we will have innovative ideas.
>
> **The second** is that by planting the seed of ranking what you would like most, you have primed your subconscious.

In response, your subconscious will hopefully start to nurture that seed without your even being aware of it.

Another Gardening Metaphor

As powerful as the subconscious is, it still needs help. If your subconscious is to watch over that seed while it turns from a seed to sapling, what will it need to help it grow? This is where you might use your list-making consciousness to help your freewheeling and mysterious subconscious. What purposeful action will you take to help achieve the negative reinforcement that comes from subtracting stress from your life?

What Needs to Go?

Finally, let's get to the title of this post. I think there is a connection between releasing a stressor or bad behavior and getting the joy of negative reinforcement. As another sophism, ask yourself *what burden or stressor you have been carrying that you would like to put down, even if only temporarily?* As you probably know, some burdens are ours to carry and...

That's life.

Have you ever carried something heavy for a while? Maybe it was something with an awkward grip, but you couldn't stop or readjust your grip? Moving furniture? Carrying too many pieces of luggage while walking to a plane? But after a while you did set the object down. Did you flex your fingers in sweet relief? That good feeling was not a reward; a reward would entail something good being added. Rather, it was negative reinforcement. It was a good feeling that came as a result of something unpleasant being removed.

Maybe, in order to get a good idea, you don't need to *add* anything. You have plenty of knowledge. You have desire and motivation. Maybe you simply need to let something go and enjoy the negative reinforcement.

TAKEAWAY FOR THIS WEEK

> We need to let go. I recently saw a catchy meme on someone's social media feed that said, "A lot of problems can be solved by removing some foods, some people, and some habits from your life." Obviously, this is overly simplistic…or is it? What if oversimplifying is the point? Find something heavy in your life. Write down what that thing(s) is. Then, put it down for a while—at least for a short while to give you some.

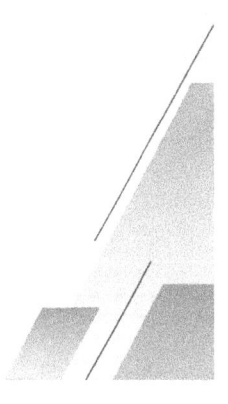

Exercise 50

WHAT IF...

*W*hat is the most important phrase you can think of? That's our first sophism of this exercise. If you skipped right to this chapter and are new to the term,

> *A sophism is a fun, relaxing creativity exercise that should push you to flex and stretch your mind.*

Let's expand this question to other groups. For an applicant, it might be one word: "Congratulations!" For those courting each other, it might be the first time that "*I love you*" is exchanged. For a sales professional the most important phrase is probably an indication that the client will buy.

Endless Possibilities

Because I am a researcher who studies creativity, I think the phrase "What if…" is the most important phrase. I find that it conveys hope and endless possibilities. And when I use the words "endless possibility," it is not meant as hyperbole; I really mean it in the literal sense.

Second sophism:

> *Find phrases that cannot go onto the end of the phrase "What if..."*

I haven't found one yet. I've even used an AI language model to test it. Basically, I'm asking you to think of what can't be thought of.

I think the magic of this phrase is that it can be used forward and backward. You could start with the end in mind. "What if I achieved my greatest desire?" What then? As you can imagine that question is a great sophism all by itself.

What Does This Have to Do with Helping People Reach Their Professional Goals and Have Revenue-Generating Ideas More Often?

WHAT IF IN PRACTICAL USE

There is no reason the phrase "what if" should not be used often in your regular sales meetings—or in any other aspect of business. In fact, try to think of a situation in your career when you shouldn't ask, "What if...?" If you are in charge, what if you had weekly "What if" sessions? What if you used "What if's" when talking to your boss? Employees? Customers?

Go back to the sophism, but this time with a twist.

> *When can't "what if" be used in business?*

TAKEAWAY FOR THIS WEEK

> I encourage you to start small. Carve out three six-minute sessions this week where you can be alone with your thoughts. It will only require a few minutes. In fact, and ironically, the difficult part always seems to be relaxing. So, build in enough time where you can slow your breathing, relax your shoulders and facial muscles, and find an alpha state. Then, grab your journal and write a list of sentences that all start with the "What if…" I think you will surprise yourself at what your subconscious will hand you.

Exercise 51

BIGGER BATTERIES

Decades ago, I bought a house at an auction. Literally. At an auction on a street, with the whole clichéd "*Going once, going twice, sold!*" thing. I was in my early twenties, and it was all I could afford. It was 900 square feet of basic living space. The 120-year-old, reclaimed hardwood floors were charming but didn't offset the fact that there was no air conditioning or even a dishwasher.

No AC?

Let me restate the fact that it didn't have air conditioning. Well, Maryland in August can easily have long heat spells with 90-degree days and humidity so thick that it feels like you are in the devil's steam bath. So, the first project I started with was hard-wiring a huge, window-based air-conditioning unit into my home's electrical system.

Increased Capacity

It took a whole weekend and too many trips to Home Depot to do it. But, with enough trial and lots and lots of errors, I got it done and, I actually learned quite a bit about electrical projects that would help me in my later efforts. One thing that stuck with me, thanks to the friendly guys at Home Depot, was that I had to be careful about the capacitor. I learned that a capacitor is like a battery. It temporarily holds a lot of electricity to basically jump-start an air conditioner when it turns on.

With regular home appliances such as lamps, the constant stream of electricity coming from an outlet is enough. With bigger appliances, such as air conditioners and refrigerators, a surge of extra electricity (such as what's stored in a capacitor) is needed to get things started.

And that leads to the first sophism:

With creativity, is our regular thinking stream enough to power the creation of innovative ideas?
Or, like a large appliance, do we need a burst from a special "creativity capacitor?"

Fast forward several decades.
I have heard the phrase "increase capacity" used more and more frequently in leadership circles when discussions turn to employee development and employee productivity.

Which brings us to producing more innovative ideas.

Can we increase the size of our creativity capacitor?

Maybe that's what's been happening in your subconscious as you have been working with these exercises. Maybe your subconscious has been building and storing creative energy. Maybe at the right moment, it will burst through with an innovative idea that simply needed more power to get going.

One more quick sophism:

If teeny, tiny bursts of electricity in the brain are related to having a good idea, what if neurons produce slightly more electricity? Would thousands of neurons producing more electricity produce a better idea?

What Does This Have to Do with Helping People Reach Their Professional Goals and Have Revenue-Generating Ideas More Often?

TAPPING THE UNTAPPED

Do your sales professionals have untapped stores of energy? Is their energy trapped in a capacitor waiting to be released? How can we get the stored creative energy out of ourselves, our workmates, and our employees? Electricity that stays stored is about as useful as a good idea that is not shared. Does your workspace have a way to get stored ideas from its employees to where those ideas need to be?

What about you?
Do you have enough (metaphorical) electricity? If you don't, how do you fill your creativity capacitor and charge your metaphorical batteries? Your answer should include more than just the largely reflexive answer of a vacation or day off from work. What are you doing with the time you already have to recharge?

Know that charging a battery isn't easy—it takes work. Have you ever felt your laptop's adaptor when it's charging? It's warm. Taking a day off can be stressful and can similarly cause excess heat. Even asking for it can cause dread in some employees. Carving out time for yourself to play with a sophism and fill your capacitor can be stressful, but the stress of having an empty capacitor is even worse.

TAKEAWAY FOR THIS WEEK

> Make time. Seven minutes, three times this week. Imagine your mind has a component that stores creative energy. Is it full? I hope so. If so, how can you increase its capacity? How can you make it store even more creative energy? As always, write or sketch your ideas. Play with these sophisms and then give your subconscious time to assemble a good idea. Not only will you be surprised by *what* it delivers to you, you will be surprised by *when* it delivers it to you.

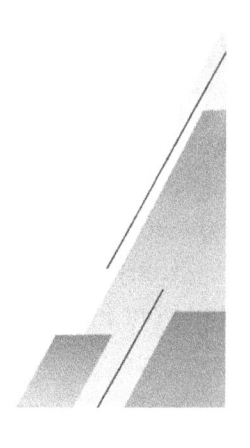

Exercise 52

BEST SONG EVER

Old Favorites

Have you ever met anyone who doesn't like music. I bet you haven't. Sure, you might have met someone who doesn't like *your* music, but they like music. You can connect with them about that. They probably even have a song they consider the best song ever.

Before we get into the best-song-ever debate, I want to ask you to reflect on something. Let me ask you to remember an old favorite song. Think back to that song that you played over and over. If you are old enough, think of that song that was on a tape that you would have to stop and rewind.

What was it about that song?

Was it the song or the way your mind created feeling when that song was playing?

Quick sophism

Try to convert your feelings about your favorite song into another domain, like smell or color? What color is your favorite song? Can you limit it to one color?

It is interesting to note that the music doesn't cause the emotion you feel when you listen to it. Your mind does. Songs don't actually exist outside of your mind. The only thing that exists outside of your mind is air vibrations. Those vibrations hit your eardrum, rattle a few things in your ear, and your subconscious somehow assembles the vibration and fluid waves as this mysterious thing called music.

Listening, Enjoying, Feeling

Those feelings about music are similar to having a good idea because they are non-conscious. Emotions and ideas come from the subconscious. *Listening* to your favorite songs is easy and automatic.

That brings us to a sophism.

Can you create your favorite song?

Why Not?

You know what you like more than some artist who you have never met does. Did a bunch of objections jump into your mind? Probably. Maybe you don't think you are musical. Maybe you don't know how to write a song. Grab your notebook or turn to the back of this book and start writing a song.

Hesitant? Scared?

Remember, we want to stretch and flex your mind.

Still Hesitant?
Fine. Jot down a title or one line. Maybe just write down what you would like your song to be about or what you want your song to make you feel. Worrying about what it will sound like, is focusing on the *product,* not the *process.* The Creativity Algorithm focuses on the process of engaging your subconscious so that it will bring you a good idea.

Slow down. Take a breath and write at least one thing that might turn into a song.

And the Best Song Ever Is?
OK, onto the part about the best song ever... I'm going to say it's John Lennon's "Imagine." "What?" How dare he say that!" I might not be a musician, but I am a psychologist who is interested in helping people reach their goals by having innovative ideas more often.

The reason I say it is the best song ever is because of the title: "Imagine" which brings us to another sophism.

Grab Your Notebook
Jot down one thing that you can't imagine. Imagination is the root of all creativity, and creativity is the source of all that is possible.

What Does This Have to Do with Helping People Reach Their Professional Goals and Have Revenue-Generating Ideas More Often?

SAME O, SAME O

Obviously, if sales professionals keep doing things the exact same way, they will keep getting the same results. Even if sales professionals consistently hit their quota, things change. Their clients' needs change. Their clients themselves change. Sales professionals will need to come up with new prospects. They will need to turn those prospects into leads and then turn those leads into sales. That will require new strategies.

Where will they get them?

From their imagination.

This exercise started with words like *feel*, *connect*, and *emotions* and that isn't an accident. Let me offer a sophism of connection. For those who are new to the Creativity Algorithm, a sophism is a mental puzzle that we play with. Playing with such a puzzle while in a relaxed alpha state will help the mind have innovative ideas more often.

OK, speaking of feelings, here's the first sophism for this week:

Would you want to feel the pain that you caused others?

Would feeling the pain that you cause others make you a better person? Would that make you closer to the person that you want to be? Would the fear of the pain you might cause others be so great that it would stop you from doing something regrettable?

Will reflecting on the sophisms in this exercise give you an innovative idea right away? Quite possibly, but this process isn't about the short term. No one can get in shape overnight. By regularly stretching and flexing your mind, creativity will flow.

Here is the second sophism for this week,

*If the best song ever was never heard,
would it still exist?*

Tweak it.

> *If the best song ever was never written,
> would it still exist.*

And again..If your conscious mind doesn't listen to the good ideas of your subconscious, do they still exist?

TAKEAWAY FOR THIS WEEK

> Too often we are product-oriented. We are also simply too rushed and focused on our to do lists. Work and family seem to require so much. The exercise for this week is to write down thoughts that come to mind after reading this exercise, even if the thoughts have nothing to do with making music or anything else in this exercise. Slow down and focus on the process. Be present and make that moment the best moment it can be.

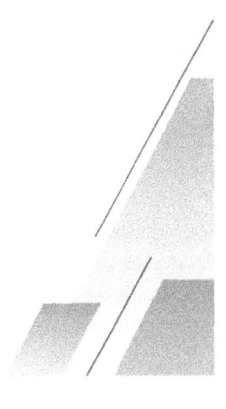

AFTERWORD

Did you notice how many times this book hinted about a future exercise or future exploration of an idea? I think the answer is six. Did you also notice that this book never quite got around to some of those exercises? That isn't a flaw. As I write this section, I could easily go back and delete any mention of a mysterious, unfulfilled future exercise.

If you are a sales professional, consider unwritten exercises as sales leads that need to be developed. Just as you wouldn't want someone else to work with the relationship you have with your clients, perhaps you wouldn't want anyone except you to develop future exercises. If you have read this far, then perhaps you see a connection between increasing the flow of your ideas and increasing sales.

Let me offer one last metaphor. Have you heard of "perpetual stew"? It is a stew that never runs dry. The recipe varies over time, as does the taste. As I understand it, the stew could be started using any recipe and any ingredients. As it gets low, more water is poured in. Different meats might be added, along with vegetables, spices, and other ingredients that might be handy. Over time the nature of the stew changes, and so does the flavor, but it is always tasty.

This is a good metaphor for the end of this book.

Good stew, innovative ideas, and good client relations take time, patience, and continual effort. Most importantly, the process is never finished but ever rewarding.

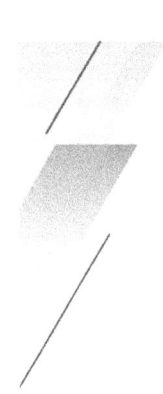

ENDNOTES

1. Huggett, Nick, "Zeno's Paradoxes". In Edward N. Zalta & Uri Nodelman (eds.), *The Stanford Encyclopedia of Philosophy*. Stanford University (Fall 2024 ed), https://plato.stanford.edu/archives/fall2024/entries/paradox-zeno/.

2. A group, unit, enterprise, etc., that is isolated from others or functions independently, typically viewed as not deriving the benefits of interrelationships or collaboration:
Silo (siloing) (n.d.) In Dictionary.com Online Dictionary. Retrieved October 16, 2024, from https://www.dictionary.com/browse/silo

3. Creativity is fascinating - why else would you be reading this book. Countless very smart PhDs have done their best to make a name for themselves and improve their career by creating a valid creativity test. No one has nailed it yet.
Abraham, A. (2018). *The Neuroscience of Creativity* (Cambridge Fundamentals of Neuroscience in Psychology), https://assets.cambridge.org/97811071/76461/frontmatter/9781107176461_frontmatter.pdf

4　Nothing can be considered creative if it is not new, or not useful.
Kaufman, J. C., & Sternberg, R. J. (2010). *The Cambridge Handbook of Creativity*. Cambridge University Press.

5　Kaufman, J. C., & Sternberg, R. J. (2010). *The Cambridge Handbook of Creativity*, Cambridge University Press.

6　A neuron receives a signal when countless molecules called neurotransmitters land on the cell. Then the cell makes a tiny electrical charge, but since neurons do not touch each other, they then spray out chemicals to other neurons down the line.
American Psychological Association. (n.d.). Alternate uses test. In *APA Dictionary of Psychology*. Retrieved December 2, 2022, from https://dictionary.apa.org/alternate-uses-test

7　Think of Big C ideas as 'disruptors." For example, Uber is a disruptor to the Taxicab industry. Uber is a Big-C idea.

8　Kaufman, J. C., & Sternberg, R. J. (2010). *The Cambridge Handbook of Creativity*. Cambridge University Press.

9　The brain is only 2% of our body's total mass, yet it consumes more energy than the thigh muscle or even the heart.
Abraham, A. (2018). *Neuroscience of Creativity*. Cambridge University Press. https://doi.org/10.1017/9781316816981

10　How would you measure a brain being "tired?" The brain has no pain receptors. When you feel tired, it is your mind doing the feeling.
Abraham, A. (2018). *Neuroscience of Creativity*. Cambridge University Press. https://doi.org/10.1017/9781316816981

11　There are different types of meditation, but unlike chemistry's periodic table of elements, the types of mediation overlap each other. Meditate to create: the impact of focused-attention and open-monitoring training on convergent and divergent thinking.
Colzato, L. S., Ozturk, A., & Hommel, B. (2012). Meditate to create: the impact of focused-attention and open-monitoring training on convergent and divergent thinking. *Frontiers in Psychology*, 3, 116. https://doi.org/10.3389/fpsyg.2012.00116

12 There is quite a bit of debate as to who should get credit. Ideas aren't one thing. Some claim credit for the name, others claim credit for putting it all into a box, and others claim credit for adding a toy.
Webly, K. (2010, April 30). The Happy Meal. *Time Magazine.* https://time.com/archive/6916040/the-happy-meal/T

13 The human brain not only wants to change, it needs to change. The brain changes slightly every time it hears, sees, smells, touches tastes or thinks something.
Beaty, R. E., Cortes, R. A., Merseal, H. M., Hardiman, M. M., & Green, A. E. (2023). Brain Networks Supporting Scientific Creative Thinking. *Psychology of Aesthetics, Creativity, and the Arts.*

14 The brain needs stimulation, that is why boredom is a stressor. Boredom is like sitting on your butt for too long. Periodically, you need to shift your weight.
Mayer, R. E.(1999). Fifty Years Of Creativity Research. In R. J. Sternberg (Ed.), *Handbook of Creativity* 449-460. Cambridge University Press.

15 Meditation requires time and effort. Getting good at meditation requires even more time and effort.
Bergland, C. (2024, March 27). Want to optimize creative flow? Practice hard then let go. *Psychology Today.*

16 Here's a secret sophism hidden at the bottom of the page, can something be creative can something be creative without change?
Hennessey, B. A., & Amabile, T. M. (2010). Creativity. *Annual Review of Psychology, 61*, 569-598. https://doi.org/10.1146/annurev.psych.093008.100416

17 Dopamine a brain chemical that is associated with wanting a reward. Dopamine makes you want a reward but dopamine levels actually dip a bit when you get the reward.
Heiss, R. (2021). *Instinct: Rewire Your Brain with Science-Backed Solutions to Increase Productivity and Achieve Success.* Citadel.

18 Clear, James, (2018). A*tomic Habits: An Easy & Proven Way to Build Good Habits & Break Bad Ones.* Penguin Publishing Group.

19 Kaufman, J. C., & Sternberg, R. J. (2010). *The Cambridge Handbook of Creativity*. Cambridge University Press.

20 Schrage, M. (2013, August 20). Just how valuable is Google's "20% time"? *Harvard Business Review*. https://hbr.org/2013/08/just-how-valuable-is-googles-2-1

21 Sekar, N. (2024, June 27). 3M's 15% rule. *Medium*. https://medium.com/@nareshnavinash/3ms-15-rule-e1bbce0b4ec5

22 Wasserman, E. A. (2023, June 20). On the origin of the Post-it Note: Intelligently designed? *Skeptical Inquirer*. https://skepticalinquirer.org/2023/06/on-the-origin-of-the-post-it-note-intelligently-designed/

23 Endestad, T., Godøy, R. I., Sneve, M. H., Hagen, T., Bochynska, A., & Laeng, B. (2020). Mental effort when playing, listening, and imagining music in one pianist's eyes and brain. *Frontiers in Human Neuroscience, 14*. https://doi.org/10.3389/fnhum.2020.576888

24 Endestad, T., Godøy, R. I., Sneve, M. H., Hagen, T., Bochynska, A., & Laeng, B. (2020). Mental effort when playing, listening, and imagining music in one pianist's eyes and brain. *Frontiers in Human Neuroscience, 14*. https://doi.org/10.3389/fnhum.2020.576888

25 Benjamin, L. T. (2014). *A Brief History of Modern Psychology*. Wiley.

26 Benjamin, L. T. (2014). *A Brief History of Modern Psychology*. Wiley.

27 Diamond, A. (2016, August 29). *"You call it procrastination, I call it thinking."* Art Diamond Blog. https://artdiamondblog.com/archives/2016/08/p_b4_1.html

28 Einstein, A. (1920). *Relativity: The special and general theory.* https://www.ibiblio.org/ebooks/Einstein/Einstein_Relativity.pdf

29 Raichle, M. E. (2015). The brain's default mode network. *Annual Review of Neuroscience, 38*(1), 433-447

30 American Psychological Association. (n.d.). *APA Dictionary of Psychology*. Retrieved December 2, 2022, from https://dictionary.apa.org/alternate-uses-test

31 Chong, A., Tolomeo, S., Yue, X., Angeles, D., Cheung, M., Benjamin, B., Lai, P. S., Lei, Z., Malavasi, F., Tang, Q., Chew, S. H., & Epstein, R. P. (2021). Blending oxytocin and dopamine with everyday creativity. *Scientific Reports, 11(1)*. https://doi.org/10.1038/s41598-021-95724-x

32 Amygdala: a ganglion of the limbic system adjoining the temporal lobe of the brain and involved in emotions of fear and aggression. Dictionary.com. (n.d.). Amygdala. In *Dictionary.com*. Retrieved October 17, 2024, from https://www.dictionary.com/browse/amygdala

33 Silver, E., & Cliburn, G. (2014, March 25). How to Change Things When Change is Hard. *Carnegie Foundation for the Advancement of Teaching*. https://www.carnegiefoundation.org/blog/how-to-change-things-when-change-is-hard/

34 Dancy, R. M. (2014). *Plato's Introduction of Forms*. Cambridge University Press.

35 American Psychological Association. (n.d.). *Apa Dictionary Of Psychology*. Retrieved December 2, 2022, from https://dictionary.apa.org/alternate-uses-test

36 American Psychological Association. (n.d.). *Apa Dictionary Of Psychology*. Retrieved December 2, 2022, from https://dictionary.apa.org/alternate-uses-test

37 A "split brain" surgery is a very rare procedure where a sufferer of severe epileptic seizures has the two hemispheres of the brain separated. There is some evidence that people who have had such surgery can think of two different thoughts simultaneously. Lienhard, D. (2017, December 27). Roger Sperry's split brain experiments (1959–1968). *The Embryo Project Encyclopedia*. Embryo.asu.edu. https://embryo.asu.edu/pages/roger-sperrys-split-brain-experiments-1959-1968-0

38 Suni, E., & Singh, A. (2023, December 8). Stages of sleep: What Happens In A Sleep Cycle. Sleep Foundation. https://www.sleepfoundation.org/stages-of-sleep

39. Bryan, L., & Peters, B. (2022, August 10). Why Do We Need sleep? *Sleep Foundation*. https://www.sleepfoundation.org/how-sleep-works/why-do-we-need-sleep

40. Cai, D. J., Mednick, S. A., Harrison, E. M., Kanady, J. C., & Mednick, S. C. (2009). REM, not incubation, improves creativity by priming associative networks. Proceedings of the *National Academy of Sciences, 106(25),* 10130–10134. https://doi.org/10.1073/pnas.0900271106

41. Cai, D. J., Mednick, S. A., Harrison, E. M., Kanady, J. C., & Mednick, S. C. (2009). REM, not incubation, improves creativity by priming associative networks. Proceedings of the *National Academy of Sciences, 106(25)*, 10130–10134. https://doi.org/10.1073/pnas.0900271106

42. Csikszentmihalyi, M. (2008). *Flow: The Psychology of Optimal Experience*. HarperCollins.

43. Watson, A. (2018, February 25). A brief guide to keeping a commonplace book. Retrieved from https://notebookofghosts.com/

44. DEVONtechnologies: Developing apps that tame the information flood, based on our own artificial intelligence technology. We all are Mac users by heart and are writing solely on the Mac and for macOS and iOS. https://www.devontechnologies.com/about

45. Hayes, S. C. (2023, March 17). The astounding number of thoughts your mind can produce. *Psychology Today*. Retrieved May 31, 2023, from https://www.psychologytoday.com/intl/blog/get-out-of-your-mind/202303/how-many-thoughts-are-in-your-head

46. Abraham, A. (2018). *Neuroscience Of Creativity*. Cambridge University Press. https://doi.org/10.1017/9781316816981

47. Abraham, A. (2018). *Neuroscience Of Creativity*. Cambridge University Press. https://doi.org/10.1017/9781316816981

48. Jäkel, S., & Dimou, L. (2017). Glial cells and their function in the adult brain: A journey through the history of their ablation. *Frontiers in Cellular Neuroscience*, 11, 24. https://doi.org/10.3389/fncel.2017.00024

49 Benjamin, L. T. (2014). *A Brief History of Modern Psychology*. Wiley.

50 Csikszentmihalyi, M. (2008). *Flow: The Psychology of Optimal Experience*. HarperCollins.

51 Rosen, D., Oh, Y., Chesebrough, C., Zhang, F., & Kounios, J. (2024). Creative flow as optimized processing: Evidence from brain oscillations during jazz improvisations by expert and non-expert musicians. *Neuropsychologia, 196*, 108824. https://doi.org/10.1016/j.neuropsychologia.2024.108824

52 Benjamin, L. T. (2014). *A Brief History of Modern Psychology*. Wiley.

53 American Psychological Association. (n.d.). A*PA Dictionary of Psychology*. Retrieved December 2, 2022, from https://dictionary.apa.org/alternate-uses-test

54 American Psychological Association. (n.d.). A*PA Dictionary of Psychology*. Retrieved December 2, 2022, from https://dictionary.apa.org/alternate-uses-test

55 Benjamin, L. T. (2014). *A Brief History of Modern Psychology*. Wiley.

56 Desautels, B. (2018, August 16). "No man ever steps in the same river twice. For it's not the same river and he's not the same man." - Heraclitus. *Bob Desautels*. https://www.bobdesautels.com/blog/2018/8/6/no-man-ever-steps-in-the-same-river-twice-for-its-not-the-same-river-and-hes-not-the-same-man-heraclitus

57 Csikszentmihalyi, M. (2008). *Flow: The Psychology of Optimal Experience*. HarperCollins.

58 Haidt, J. (2012). *The Righteous Mind: Why good people are divided by politics and religion.* Pantheon Books

59 Best, K. (2018, August 7). Know Thyself: The philosophy of self-knowledge. *UConn Today*. https://today.uconn.edu/2018/08/know-thyself-philosophy-self-knowledge/

60 Cameron, J. (2016). *The Artist's Way: 30th Anniversary Edition*. Penguin Publishing Group.

61 Davis, S. (2023, March 9). New year's resolutions statistics (2023) – Forbes Health. *Forbes*. Retrieved August 19, 2023, from https://www.forbes.com/health/mind/new-years-resolutions-statistics/

62 Loftus, E. (2019, October). How memory can be manipulated (K. Luna, Interviewer) [Interview]. In *Speaking of Psychology* podcast. American Psychological Association. https://www.apa.org/news/podcasts/speaking-of-psychology/memory-manipulated

63 Loftus, E. (2019, October). How memory can be manipulated (K. Luna, Interviewer) [Interview]. In *Speaking of Psychology* podcast. American Psychological Association. https://www.apa.org/news/podcasts/speaking-of-psychology/memory-manipulated

64 Kaufield, K. (2014, June 30). Dropping my daughter off at camp taught me how to let go. *HuffPost*. https://www.huffpost.com/archive/ca/entry/dropping-my-daughter-off-at-camp-taught-me-how-to-let-go_b_5542346

65 Zhang, J. (2019). Basic neural units of the brain: Neurons, synapses, and action potential. arXiv. https://arxiv.org/abs/1906.01703

66 L'Engle, M. (1962). *A Wrinkle in Time* (Murry family series, v.1). Dell.

67 Im, K., Lee, J.-M. ., Lyttelton, O., Kim, S. H., Evans, A. C., & Kim, S. I. (2008). Brain Size and Cortical Structure in the Adult Human Brain. *Cerebral Cortex, 18*(9), 2181–2191. https://doi.org/10.1093/cercor/bhm244

68 Beaty, R. E., & Kenett, Y. N. (2023). Associative thinking at the core of creativity. *Trends in Cognitive Science, 10*(10).

69 Parker, N. (2020, December 11). The Angel in the Marble. *Medium*. https://nilsaparker.medium.com/the-angel-in-the-marble-f7aa43f333dc

70 Zoomies: a slang term for a sudden burst of hyperactivity by a dog, cat, or other animal—such as rapidly running back and forth or in circles. The term is typically applied to pets, as opposed to wild animals.
Dictionary.com. (n.d.). Zoomies. In *Dictionary.com*. Retrieved [October 16, 2024], from https://www.dictionary.com/e/zoomies

71 American Psychological Association. (n.d.). *APA Dictionary Of Psychology*. Retrieved December 2, 2022, from https://dictionary.apa.org/alternate-uses-testt

72 American Psychological Association. (n.d.). *APA Dictionary Of Psychology*. Retrieved December 2, 2022, from https://dictionary.apa.org/alternate-uses-test

73 American Psychological Association. (n.d.). *Apa Dictionary Of Psychology*. Retrieved December 2, 2022, from https://dictionary.apa.org/alternate-uses-test

74 Debbie_Downer: A fictional Saturday Night Live character who debuted in 2004, and eventually became an established slang phrase referring to a pessimistic person who frequently adds bad news and negative feelings to a gathering, thus bringing down the mood of everyone around them.
Wikipedia contributors. (n.d.). Debbie Downer. In Wikipedia, The Free Encyclopedia. Retrieved [October 16, 2024], from https://en.wikipedia.org/wiki/Debbie_Downer

75 Simply Psychology. (n.d.). Negative reinforcement. Retrieved [October 16, 2024], from https://www.simplypsychology.org/negative-reinforcement.html

76 Simply Psychology. (n.d.). Negative reinforcement. Retrieved [October 16, 2024], from https://www.simplypsychology.org/negative-reinforcement.html

77 Endorphins are hormones that are released when your body feels pain or stress. They are produced in your brain and act as messengers in your body. Endorphins are produced to help relieve pain, reduce stress and improve mood. Endorphins can be boosted by exercising, eating, having sex, getting a massage and many other ways.
Cleveland Clinic. (n.d.). Endorphins. Retrieved [October 16, 2024], from https://my.clevelandclinic.org/health/body/23040-endorphins

REFERENCES

A.P.A. Psychology. (n.d.). *APA Dictionary of Psychology*. Retrieved December 2, 2022, from https://dictionary.apa.org/alternate-uses-test

Abraham, A. (2018). *Neuroscience of Creativity*. Cambridge University Press. https://doi.org/10.1017/9781316816981

Alanson, C. (2017). *Black Ops*. Createspace.

Alper, M. (2008). *God Part of the Brain: A Scientific Interpretation of Human Spirituality and God*. Sourcebooks.

Anderson, C. (2016). *TED Talks: The Official TED Guide to Public Speaking*. Houghton Mifflin Harcourt.

Astore, R. (n.d.). *Spinoza on God Affects and the Nature of Sorrow*. Florida Philosophical Review, College of Arts and Humanities. Retrieved December 26, 2023, from https://cah.ucf.edu/fpr/article/spinoza-on-god-affects-and-the-nature-of-sorrow/

Beaty, R. E., & Kenett, Y. N. (2023). Associative thinking at the core of creativity. *Trends in Cognitive Science, 10*(10).

Beaty, R. E., Cortes, R. A., Merseal, H. M., Hardiman, M. M., & Green, A. E. (2023). Brain networks supporting scientific creative thinking. *Psychology of Aesthetics, Creativity, and the Arts*.

Benjamin, L. T. (2014). *A Brief History of Modern Psychology*. Wiley.

Bergland, C. (2024, March 27). Want to optimize creative flow? Practice hard then let go. *Psychology Today*.

Beutell, C. (2022, December 15). *Health benefits of having a routine*. https://www.nm.org/healthbeat/healthy-tips/health-benefits-of-having-a-routine#:=An%20effective%20routine%20can%20helpemotional%20well%2Dbeing%20and%20energy

Bhaskar, S., Hemavathy, D., & Prasad, S. (2016). Prevalence of chronic insomnia in adult patients and its correlation with medical comorbidities. *Journal of Family Medicine and Primary Care, 5*(4), 780-784.

Bilalić, M., McLeod, P., & Gobet, F. (2010). The mechanism of the Einstellung (set) effect: A pervasive source of cognitive bias. *Current Directions in Psychological Science, 19*(2), 111-115. https://doi.org/10.1177/0963721410363571

Bolia, B., Jha, S., & Jha, M. (2016). Cognitive dissonance: A review of causes and marketing implications. *Researchers World, 7*, 63-76. https://doi.org/10.18843/RWJASC/V7I2/06

Brenner, C. B., & Zacks, J. M. (2011, December 13). Why walking through a doorway makes you forget. *Scientific American*. Retrieved January 16, 2023, from https://www.scientificamerican.com/article/why-walking-through-doorway-makes-you-forget/

Burkus, D. (2013). *The Myths of Creativity: The Truth About How Innovative Companies and People Generate Great Ideas*. Jossey-Bass.

Cameron, J. (2016). *The Artist's Way: 30th Anniversary Edition*. Penguin Publishing Group.

Candle problem. (n.d.). *Wikipedia*. Retrieved December 22, 2022, from https://en.wikipedia.org/wiki/Candle_problem

Cherry, K. (2022, May 7). Procedural memory: Definition, examples, and how it works. *Verywell Mind*. Retrieved January 15, 2023, from https://www.verywellmind.com/what-is-procedural-memory-2795478

Chong, A., Tolomeo, S., Yue, X., Angeles, D., Cheung, M., Benjamin, B., Lai, P. S., Lei, Z., Malavasi, F., Tang, Q., Chew, S. H., & Epstein, R. P. (2021). Blending oxytocin and dopamine with everyday creativity. *Scientific Reports, 11*(1). https://doi.org/10.1038/s41598-021-95724-x

Clear, J. (2018). *Atomic Habits: An Easy & Proven Way to Build Good Habits & Break Bad Ones*. Penguin Publishing Group.

Csikszentmihalyi, M. (2008). *Flow: The Psychology of Optimal Experience*. HarperCollins.

Dabrowski, J., & Reed-Marshall, T. (2018, November). Motivation and engagement in student assignments: The role of choice and relevancy. *Equity in Motion, 1-14*.

Dancy, R. M. (2014). *Plato's Introduction of Forms*. Cambridge University Press.

Davis, S. (2023, March 9). New year's resolutions statistics (2023) – Forbes Health. *Forbes*. Retrieved August 19, 2023, from https://www.forbes.com/health/mind/new-years-resolutions-statistics/

Development of the periodic table. (n.d.). *The Royal Society of Chemistry*. Retrieved May 30, 2023, from https://www.rsc.org/periodic-table/history/about

Dormhoff, G. W., & Fox, K. C. R. (2015, May). Dreaming and the default network: A review, synthesis, and counterintuitive research proposal. *Consciousness and Cognition, 33*, 342-355. https://doi.org/10.1016/j.concog.2015.01.019

Endestad, T., Godøy, R. I., Sneve, M. H., Hagen, T., Bochynska, A., & Laeng, B. (2020). Mental effort when playing, listening, and imagining music in one pianist's eyes and brain. *Frontiers in Human Neuroscience, 14*. https://doi.org/10.3389/fnhum.2020.576888

Epstein, D. (2019). *Range: Why Generalists Triumph in a Specialized World*. Penguin Publishing Group.

Feist, G. (1998). A meta-analysis of personality in scientific and artistic creativity. *Personality and Social Psychology Review, 2*, 290-309. https://doi.org/10.1207/s15327957pspr0204_5

Fredericks, A. (2022). *From Fizzle to Sizzle: The Hidden Forces Crushing Your Creativity and How You Can Overcome Them*. Blue River Books.

Frith, E., Ponce, P., & Loprinzi, P. D. (2019). Active or inert? An experimental comparison of creative ideation across incubation periods. *Journal of Creative Behavior, 55*(1), 5-14. https://doi.org/10.1002/jocb.429

Gilbert, E. (2016). *Big Magic: Creative Living Beyond Fear*. Penguin Publishing Group.

Glowatz, E. (2016, November 8). Do you struggle with multitasking? Why the brain can only focus on one thing at a time. *Medical Daily*. Retrieved January 15, 2023, from https://www.medicaldaily.com/do-you-struggle-multitasking-why-brain-can-only-focus-one-thing-time-403792

Greenfield, S. (2016). *Mind Change: How Digital Technologies are Leaving Their Mark on Our Brains*. Random House.

Grivas, M. (2018). *Think and Discover: Build Your Creative Confidence*. 7 Cs Life.

Guilford, J. P. (1950). Creativity. *American Psychologist, 5*, 444-454. https://doi.org/10.1037/h0063487

Hennessey, B. A., & Amabile, T. M. (2010). Creativity. *Annual Review of Psychology, 61*, 569-598. https://doi.org/10.1146/annurev.psych.093008.100416

Heiss, R. (2021). Instinct: Rewire Your Brain with Science-Backed Solutions to Increase Productivity and Achieve Success. Citadel.

Jablokow, K. W., & Booth, D. E. (2006). The impact and management of cognitive gap in high performance product development organizations. *Journal of Engineering and Technology Management, 23*(4), 313-336. https://doi.org/10.1016/j.jengtecman.2006.08.002

James, W. (1907). *Pragmatism: A New Name for Some Old Ways of Thinking*. Longmans, Green, and Co.

Johansson, F. (2006). *The Medici Effect: What Elephants and Epidemics Can Teach Us About Innovation*. Harvard Business Review Press.

REFERENCES

Kaufman, S. B. (2020). *Transcend: The New Science of Self-Actualization*. Penguin Publishing Group.

Kaufman, S. B., & Gregoire, C. (2015). *Wired to Create: Unraveling the Mysteries of the Creative Mind*. Penguin Publishing Group.

Kaufman, J. C., & Sternberg, R. J. (2010). The Cambridge Handbook of Creativity. *Cambridge University Press*.

Kouzes, J. M., & Posner, B. Z. (2002). *The Leadership Challenge: How to Keep Getting Extraordinary Things Done in Organizations*. John Wiley & Sons.

Kraus, A. (n.d.). *Kraus group: Improving your people for better performance*. Retrieved January 15, 2023, from https://krausgroup.com

Kurtzberg, T. R., & Amabile, T. M. (2001). From Guilford to creative synergy: Opening the black box of team-level creativity. *Creativity Research Journal, 13*(3-4), 285-294. https://doi.org/10.1207/S15326934CRJ1334_06

Langer, E. J. (1990). Mindfulness. *Daedalus, 119*(1), 189-206.

Larkin, K. (2021, May 5). From the archive: The cosmic om. *The Irish Times*. Retrieved June 2, 2023, from https://www.irishtimes.com/life-and-style/people/from-the-archive-the-cosmic-om-1.4607874

Leonard, K. (2020, March 3). 9 tips for better time management. *Forbes*. Retrieved February 7, 2023, from https://www.forbes.com/sites/forbescoachescouncil/2020/03/03/9-tips-for-better-time-management/

Logan, G. D. (1988). Toward an instance theory of automatization. *Psychological Review, 95*(4), 492-527. https://doi.org/10.1037/0033-295X.95.4.492

Lu, C. (2023, January 3). The secret to solving hard problems? Brainstorm in groups of three. *Science.org*. Retrieved August 3, 2023, from https://www.science.org/content/article/secret-solving-hard-problems-brainstorm-groups-three

Mayer, R. E. (1999). Fifty years of creativity research. In R. J. Sternberg (Ed.), *Handbook of Creativity* (pp. 449-460). Cambridge University Press.

Meninger, M. (2014). Creativity development: Children with disabilities in an inclusive early childhood education program. *International Journal of Inclusive Education, 18*(11), 1193-1211. https://doi.org/10.1080/13603116.2014.885592

Metzl, E. S. (2009). The role of creative thinking in resilience after Hurricane Katrina. *Psychology of Aesthetics, Creativity, and the Arts, 3*(2), 112-123. https://doi.org/10.1037/a0013479

Mumford, M. D., Connelly, M. S., & Gaddis, B. (2003). How creative leaders think: Experimental findings and cases. *Leadership Quarterly, 14*(4-5), 411-432. https://doi.org/10.1016/S1048-9843(03)00045-6

Necka, E. (2003). *Creative Interaction: A Conceptual Schema for the Process-Oriented Approach*. Wydawnictwo UMCS.

Nestle, M. (2013). *Food Politics: How the Food Industry Influences Nutrition and Health*. University of California Press.

Nielsen, L. A., & Thurber, J. S. (2016). *The Secret of Teams: What Great Teams Know and Do*. Berrett-Koehler Publishers.

Nisbett, R. E., & Ross, L. (1980). *Human Inference: Strategies and Shortcomings of Social Judgment*. Prentice-Hall.

Noe, A. (2006). *Action in Perception*. The MIT Press.

Pennebaker, J. W. (1997). *Opening Up: The Healing Power of Expressing Emotions*. Guilford Press.

Phillips, L. (2019, February 19). Practicing mindfulness can help you find balance in life. *The Conversation*. Retrieved January 15, 2023, from https://theconversation.com/practicing-mindfulness-can-help-you-find-balance-in-life-109891

Plucker, J. A., Beghetto, R. A., & Dow, G. T. (2004). Why isn't creativity more important to educational psychologists? Potentials, pitfalls, and future directions in creativity research. *Educational Psychologist, 39*(2), 83-96. https://doi.org/10.1207/s15326985ep3902_1

Poetker, B. (2023, April 18). What is workplace culture? *G2.com*. Retrieved August 4, 2023, from https://www.g2.com/articles/workplace-culture

Rathunde, K. (2015). The experience of learning in Montessori classrooms. In N. Budwig, E. Turiel, & P. D. Zelazo (Eds.), *New Perspectives on Human Development* (pp. 129-153). Cambridge University Press.

Reivich, K., & Shatté, A. (2002). *The Resilience Factor: 7 Essential Skills for Overcoming Life's Inevitable Obstacles*. Broadway Books.

Roberto, M. A. (2019) *Unlocking Creativity: How to Solve Any Problem and Make the Best Decisions by Shifting Creative Mindsets*. Wiley.

Robinson, K. (2011). *Out of Our Minds: Learning to Be Creative*. Wiley.

Runco, M. A. (2007). *Creativity: Theories and Themes: Research, Development, and Practice*. Elsevier Academic Press.

Runco, M. A., & Acar, S. (2012). Divergent thinking as an indicator of creative potential. *Creativity Research Journal, 24*(1), 66-75. https://doi.org/10.1080/10400419.2012.652929

Sawyer, R. K. (2006). *Explaining Creativity: The Science of Human Innovation*. Oxford University Press.

Scalzo, R. (2017). *Habits of Highly Creative People: 10 Tips to Help You Succeed*. Creative Communications.

Schmid, K. (2021). *The Creative Architect: Learning from Frank Lloyd Wright*. University of Chicago Press.

Simonton, D. K. (2000). Creative development as acquired expertise: Theoretical issues and an empirical test. *Developmental Review, 20*(2), 283-318. https://doi.org/10.1006/drev.1999.0504

Simonton, D. K. (2013). Creative thought as blind-variation and selective-retention: Combinatorial models of exceptional creativity. *Physics of Life Reviews, 10*(2), 239-271. https://doi.org/10.1016/j.plrev.2013.03.005

Simonton, D. K. (2021). Thematic content analysis of insight: Blind variation, selective retention, and the patterns of creative thought. *Journal of Creative Behavior, 55*(4), 883-897. https://doi.org/10.1002/jocb.469

Simon, H. A. (1985). *Models of Bounded Rationality*. The MIT Press.

Sio, U. N., & Ormerod, T. C. (2009). Does incubation enhance problem solving? A meta-analytic review. *Psychological Bulletin, 135*(1), 94-120. https://doi.org/10.1037/a0014212

Sobel, D. (2017). *The Glass Universe: How the Ladies of the Harvard Observatory Took the Measure of the Stars*. Penguin Publishing Group.

Sternberg, R. J. (1985). *Beyond IQ: A Triarchic Theory of Human Intelligence*. Cambridge University Press.

Sternberg, R. J. (2019). *The Theory of Successful Intelligence*. Springer.

Sternberg, R. J., & Lubart, T. I. (1991). An investment theory of creativity and its development. *Human Development, 34*(1), 1-31. https://doi.org/10.1159/000277029

Sternberg, R. J., & Lubart, T. I. (1995). *Defying the Crowd: Cultivating Creativity in a Culture of Conformity*. Free Press.

Sternberg, R. J., & Williams, W. M. (1996). *How to Develop Student Creativity*. Association for Supervision and Curriculum Development.

Tharp, T., & Reiter, M. (2006). *The Creative Habit: Learn It and Use It for Life*. Simon & Schuster.

Tharp, T., & Reiter, M. (2013). *The Collaborative Habit: Life Lessons for Working Together*. Simon & Schuster.

Thomas, J. B., Clark, S. M., & Gioia, D. A. (1993). Strategic sensemaking and organizational performance: Linkages among scanning, interpretation, action, and outcomes. *Academy of Management Journal, 36*(2), 239-270. https://doi.org/10.2307/256522

Tobias, C. U. (2022). *Enhancing Creativity in the Classroom: A Teacher's Guide*. Teachers College Press.

Ulrich, D. (2015). *HR from the Outside In: Six Competencies for the Future of Human Resources*. McGraw-Hill Education.

Ulrich, R. (1984). View through a window may influence recovery from surgery. *Science, 224*(4647), 420-421. https://doi.org/10.1126/science.6143402

von Thienen, J., Meinel, C., & Nicolai, C. (2014). How design thinking tools help to solve wicked problems. In *Design Thinking Research* (pp. 97-104). Springer. https://doi.org/10.1007/978-3-319-01303-9_6

Wallas, G. (1926). *The Art of Thought*. Harcourt Brace.

Weisberg, R. W. (1993). *Creativity: Beyond the Myth of Genius*. W. H. Freeman.

Weisberg, R. W. (2020). *Rethinking Creativity: Inside-the-Box Thinking as the Basis for Innovation*. Cambridge University Press.

West, R. L., & Stanovich, K. E. (2003). Is the conjunction fallacy tied to probabilistic reasoning? *Memory & Cognition, 31*(5), 763-773. https://doi.org/10.3758/BF03196117

Williams, K. M., Nathanson, C., & Paulus, P. B. (2003). Dynamics of idea generation in groups. In P. B. Paulus & B. A. Nijstad (Eds.), *Group Creativity: Innovation through Collaboration* (pp. 115-138). Oxford University Press.

Williams, W. M., & Yang, L. T. (1999). Organizational creativity. In R. J. Sternberg (Ed.), *Handbook of Creativity* (pp. 373-391). Cambridge University Press.

Wilson, J. M. (2014, April 14). *How creativity builds resilience in youth*. UAB News. Retrieved August 22, 2023, from https://www.uab.edu/news/youcanuse/item/4326-how-creativity-builds-resilience-in-youth

Witt, L. A. (2006). The interactive effects of extraversion and conscientiousness on performance. *Journal of Management, 32*(5), 805-831. https://doi.org/10.1177/0149206306292516

Woods, T. (2021). *Brainstorming Techniques: The Power of Divergent Thinking*. Ideapress Publishing.

Wright, F. L. (1954). *The Natural House*. Horizon Press.

Wroblewski, L. (2022). *Web Form Design: Filling in the Blanks*. Rosenfeld Media.

Wulf, M. A., & Lewin, K. (1994). *Resolving Social Conflicts and Field Theory in Social Science*. American Psychological Association.

Young, J. W. (2003). *A Technique for Producing Ideas*. McGraw-Hill Education.

Zohar, D., & Marshall, I. (2000). *SQ: Connecting with Our Spiritual Intelligence*. Bloomsbury.

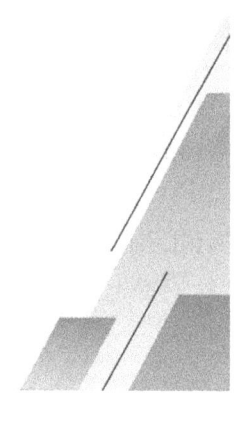

Notes

Notes

Notes

Notes

Notes

Notes